ROAD TRANSPORT RESEARCH

ORGANISATION FOR ECONOMIC CO-OPERATION AND DEVELOPMENT

Pursuant to article 1 of the Convention signed in Paris on 14th December 1960, and which came into force on 30th September 1961, the Organisation for Economic Co-operation and Development (OECD) shall promote policies designed:

- to achieve the highest sustainable economic growth and employment and a rising standard of living in Member countries, while maintaining financial stability, and thus to contribute to the development of the world economy;
- to contribute to sound economic expansion in Member as well as non-member countries in the process of economic development; and
- to contribute to the expansion of world trade on a multilateral, non-discriminatory basis in accordance with international obligations.

The original Member countries of the OECD are Austria, Belgium, Canada, Denmark, France, the Federal Republic of Germany, Greece, Iceland, Ireland, Italy, Luxembourg, the Netherlands, Norway, Portugal, Spain, Sweden, Switzerland, Turkey, the United Kingdom and the United States. The following countries became Members subsequently through accession at the dates indicated hereafter: Japan (28th April 1964), Finland (28th January 1969), Australia (7th June 1971) and New Zealand (29th May 1973).

The Socialist Federal Republic of Yugoslavia takes part in some of the work of the OECD (agreement of 28th October 1961).

Publié en français sous le titre :

**ADAPTATIONS DU COMPORTEMENT
AUX CHANGEMENTS DANS LE SYSTÈME
DE TRANSPORTS ROUTIERS**

FOREWORD

The Programme centres on road and road transport research, while taking into account the impacts of intermodal aspects on the road transport system as a whole. It is geared towards a technico-economic approach to solving key road transport issues identified by Member countries. The Programme has two main fields of activity:

-- The international co-operation in road and road transport research to provide scientific support for decisions by Member governemnts and international governmental organisations, and to assess future strategies concerning roads and road transport problems and the priority policy concerns of Member countries;

-- The information and documentation programme (IRRD -- International Road Research Documentation), a co-operative scheme that provides a mechanism for the systematic world-wide exchange of information on scientific literature and current research programmes.

The scientific and technical activities concern:

-- The assessment of urban and inter-urban road transport strategies;

-- The development and management of road traffic control and driver communication systems to enhance network efficiency and quality of services;

-- The formulation and evaluation of integrated road and traffic safety programmes;

-- The construction, preservation and rehabilitation of road infrastructure.

-- The maintenance management of road infrastructure and the evaluation of traffic safety measures and strategies in developing countries.

ABSTRACT

IRRD No. 824028

The report was prepared by an International Scientific Expert Group of the OECD Road Transport Research Programme. The study started in September 1987 and its aim was to review safety issues related to behavioural adaption which may occur following the introduction of safety improvements to the road transport system. The report is organised in eight chapters : 1. Introduction, 2. Definitions and Issues, 3. Highway Safety, 4. Vehicle Safety, 5. Education and Enforcement, 6. Review of Theoretical Literature, 7. Methodological Issues, 8. Conclusions and Recommendations. It provides an evaluation of theories and models of driver behaviour as well as explanations on the effects of behavioural adaptation on the efficiency of road safety programmes. Practical recommendations are developed to provide concrete guidelines for road safety administrators, programme planners and researchers, and to stimulate new research on road user behaviour.

Subject Classification: 83, 82.

Fields: Accidents and the human factor, accidents and the road.

Keywords: Adaptation (psychol), behaviour, design (overall design), driver, education, highway design, layout, legislation, mathematical model, modification, psychology, publicity, road user, safety, vehicle.

Purpose

Behavioural adaptations of road users which may occur following the introduction of safety measures in the transport system are of particular concern to road authorities, regulatory bodies and motor vehicle manufacturers particularly in cases where such adaptations may decrease the expected safety benefits.

This study was undertaken by a Scientific Expert Group from 16 OECD Member Countries with the aim of reviewing to what extent and in what direction drivers adjust their behaviour in response to system changes which are designated to improve safety The effect of behavioural adaptation can range from an improved safety benefit to no change in the safety to a negative effect on safety. Based on a survey of Member countries and the scientific literature available, the report provides an evaluation of this issue, including the extent to which this phenomenon may or may not exist, techniques used or proposed to measure it, and the implications on how to estimate and assess countermeasure effectiveness.

Definition

"Behavioural adaptation" was selected as the label to describe the types of behavioural changes of concern in the report. The label was selected because it does not make reference to any of the current explanations for the unintended behavioural adaptations which occur following changes to the road transport system. Although the label is convenient for the purposes of the report, it is not without its problems because adaptation has different meanings in fields such as perception, learning and social psychology.

Therefore on the full report an explanation of behavioural adaptation is presented along with a discussion of some of the important issues related to it. The issues discussed include the epistemological basis for the term, the use of retrospective analyses to support its existence, the use of accident and fatality data versus behavioural data for evaluating road safety programmes, the spatial and temporal limits of behavioural adaptation, and the adaptation of road users to non-safety changes in the road transport system.

Research Assessment

The report contains descriptions of research studies in which behavioural adaptation has been observed, including roadway and vehicle feature changes as well as well as publicity campaigns, education and training programmes. Research related to the roadway is reviewed, referring to examples of how drivers have adapted to a number of roadway changes such as centre and edge line markings, lighting, shoulder and lane width, and improvements to intersection sight distances. In general, roadway changes indicate that although drivers may make some adaptations there usually remains a net safety benefit.

Research describing how road users adapt to changes in the vehicle is based on results of studies on vehicle features such as studded tyres, antilock brake systems, daytime running lights, and seat belts. The results indicate that frequently road users adapt to the changes, but there is a range of effects observed. It is noted that those safety measures which potentially increase the mobility of drivers may be most prone to the influence of behavioural adaptation.

Research on road safety publicity campaigns, education and training programmes, and road safety legislation is of major importance. However, the lack of behavioural data makes it difficult to determine if behavioural adaptation is a problem for these types of programmes. It is suggested that the nature of the change process resulting from publicity and education campaigns might preclude adaptation by those who are influenced by it, but other road users may be forced to change their behaviours to deal with changes brought about by the education and publicity.

Models and Methodologies

In order to establish a frame of reference for organising the information about behavioural adaptation, a number of models and theories of road user behaviour which suggest the existence of behavioural adaptation are reviewed. Each of these provides a different explanation for why road users change their behaviour in response to changes in the transport system.

Because of the complexity of the subject area and the wider context covering these questions, the report provides a summary of the methodological problems involved with studying behavioural adaptation. This should also provide useful information for those practitioners and researchers who wish to incorporate the study of behavioural adaptation into their programmes and research.

Contents

The study report is organised in eight chapters. It discusses the problem identification in Chapter I; presents definitions and issues associated with behavioural adaptation in Chapter II; reviews the impacts on various user categories of major road and environment safety improvements in Chapter III, examines the effects of technical progress in the vehicle sector on driver behaviour in Chapter IV; provides an evaluation of education and training programmes attempting to modify road user behaviour by means of legislation and enforcement in Chapter V; reviews past and current literature in order to better understand behavioural theories and models in Chapter VI; identifies the problems involved from a methodological point of view in Chapter VII; and summarises research needs, conclusions and recommendations in Chapter VIII.

Key Conclusion

An important conclusion of the Scientific Expert Group is that behavioural adaptation exists, and does have an effect on the safety benefits achieved through road safety programmes. Results indicate that, generally, behavioural adaptation does not eliminate the safety gains obtained, but it does reduce the effectiveness of road safety programmes in a number of cases. A series of recommendations are presented for continued research into the effects of behavioural adaptation on road safety programmes and for the development of a better understanding of the process of behaviour change following the introduction of road safety initiatives.

In view of the relative novelty and scarcity of comprehensive research and widely accepted evidence in this sector, the Group wishes to emphasize the importance of increasing research investments on human behavioural sciences to advance the state-of-the-art of road traffic safety against the background of diminishing returns of specific road accident countermeasures. The study should provide a framework for practitioners and researchers to incorporate the concept of behavioural adaptation into road safety policy actions and research programmes.

Also available

ROAD SAFETY: MEASURES PROGRAMMES AND GUIDELINES

INTEGRATED TRAFFIC SAFETY MANAGEMENT IN URBAN AREAS (1990)
(77 89 06 1) ISBN 92-64-13317-8 122 pp.   £13.00   US$25.00   FF120   DM47

CURTAILING USAGE OF DE-ICING AGENTS IN WINTER MAINTENANCE
(1989)
(77 89 04 1) ISBN 92-64-13280-5 124 pp.   £13.50   US$24.00   FF110   DM46

TRAFFIC MANAGEMENT AND SAFETY AT HIGHWAY WORK ZONES
(1989)
(77 89 03 1) ISBN 92-64-13281-3 146 pp.   £17.00   US$30.00   FF140   DM58

ROAD ACCIDENTS: ON-SITE INVESTIGATIONS (1988)
(77 88 02 1) ISBN 982-64-13044-6 104 pp.   £8.80   US$16.50   FF75   DM32

TRANSPORTING HAZARDOUS GOODS BY ROAD (1988)
(77 88 03 1) ISBN 92-64-13051-9 146 pp.   £11.20   US$21.00   FF95   DM41

EFFECTIVENESS OF ROAD SAFETY EDUCATION PROGRAMMES (1986)
(77 86 03 1) ISBN 92-64-12881-6 134 pp.   £7.50   US$15.00   FF75   DM33

OECD ROAD SAFETY RESEARCH: A SYNTHESIS (1986)
(77 86 01 1) ISBN 92-64-12814-X 106 pp.   £6.00   US$12.00   FF60   DM27

GUIDELINES FOR IMPROVING THE SAFETY OF ELDERLY ROAD USERS
(1896)
38 pages, free on request from OECD

TRAFFIC SAFETY OF ELDERLY ROAD USERS. Report Prepared for OECD
and WHO (1985)
(77 85 03 1) ISBN 92-64-12756-9 184 pp.   £7.50   US$15.00   FF75   DM33

INTEGRATED ROAD SAFETY PROGRAMMES (1984)
(77 84 03 1) ISBN 92-64-12620-1 96 pp.   £5.90   US$12.00   FF59   DM26

TRAFFIC SAFETY OF CHILDREN (1983)
(77 83 02 1) ISBN 92-64-12468-3 110 pp.   £6.50   US$13.00   FF65   DM29

Prices charged at the OECD Bookshop.

*The OECD CATALOGUE OF PUBLICATIONS and supplements will be sent free of charge
on request addressed either to OECD Publications Service,
2, rue André-Pascal, 75775 PARIS CEDEX 16, or to the OECD Distributor in your country.*

TABLE OF CONTENTS

Chapter VII

METHODOLOGICAL ISSUES 105

Chapter VIII

CONCLUSIONS AND RECOMMENDATIONS 115

LIST OF GROUP MEMBERS 121

Chapter I

INTRODUCTION

Developing road safety programmes (*) which will successfully reduce the number of road users who are killed or injured is a complex process which requires the evaluation of many variables, especially roadway environments, vehicles, and road users. Equally important is the need to consider how these components of the system interact with each other to create the traffic environment. Consideration of the interaction between the elements will lead to more effective programmes, which, as a consequence, will produce a safer road transport system. Safety programmes, whether directed at the road system, the vehicle or the road user, are generally very costly, and therefore there is a definite economic benefit to be derived from developing those programmes which produce the best overall gains in safety.

I.1. PURPOSE OF THE REPORT

The purpose of the report is to examine evidence of road user behaviours which occur in response to road safety programmes and to assess the potential impact of these behaviours on the safety benefits obtained from the programmes. The objectives of the report are:

1. To define behavioural adaptation;

2. To review the issues associated with the phenomena;

3. To review research which describes the responses of road users to road safety programmes directed at the highway system, the vehicle and road users;

---

* A road safety programme is defined as an activity which is designed to improve the overall safety of the transportation system. It may, therefore, include changes which affect the safety of the motor vehicle, the road system, or road users.

4. To review the theories of road user behaviour which might explain the phenomena;

5. To discuss methodological issues associated with research about the phenomena;

6. To provide conclusions about the existence, extent, and magnitude of the phenomena;

7. To provide recommendations for the consideration of the phenomena in research.

I.2.   BEHAVIOURAL ADAPTATION

"Behavioural adaptation" was selected as the label to describe the types of behavioural changes of concern in the report. The label was selected because it does not make reference to any of the current explanations for the unintended behavioural adaptations which occur following changes to the road transportation system. Although the label is convenient for the purposes of the report, it is not without its problems because adaptation has different meanings in fields such as perception, learning, and social psychology.

Behavioural adaptation is a term used to describe those behaviours which may occur following the introduction of changes to the road-vehicle-user system and which are not consistent with the initial purpose of the change, unless behavioural adaptation has been accounted for in advance. These behavioural changes allow road users to use the system changes to satisfy their needs, and as a result the changes produce a continuum of effects ranging from a positive increase in safety to a decrease in safety. The definition is specific to road safety and is not necessarily consistent with definitions of adaptation used in other disciplines.

Behavioural adaptation is observed when engineers, programmers, and others make changes in the transportation system, and road users change their behaviour in a manner inconsistent with the goals of those initiating the change. In general, if road users continued to act as they had before the change occurred, we would anticipate a safety or mobility benefit from the change. However, it has been observed in a number of cases that safety measures, which should have resulted in a decrease in accidents and fatalities, have failed to produce the desired effect. Although there may have been an improvement in safety, the effect may not be as great as had been anticipated. It is hypothesized that the failure of the change to produce the desired result may be due to changes in the behaviour of road users. These changes in behaviour may occur because road users attempt to achieve their own goals, which may not be consistent with those of the planners.

Although behavioural adaptation is likely to occur among all groups of road users, the one group most likely to influence fatality rates is drivers. Research presented in the report will concentrate on the driver, but the conclusions and discussions are also applicable to other road users, and, where available, examples of the behaviour of other road users will be cited. Adams (7), after reviewing data at the aggregate level, gives a number of examples of how other road users adapt to changes in the road system. As well, he argues that many changes which improve the safety of vehicles tend to shift the burden of risk from the driver, and vehicle occupant, to less powerful (politically) and less protected groups such as pedestrians and cyclists.

I.3. CONTROVERSY

The report was initiated, in part, as a result of a debate in the scientific literature about the usefulness of road safety programmes. Some researchers have argued that the responses of road users to safety improvements could eliminate all positive benefits of road safety programmes. There is evidence that road users do, at times, change their behaviour in unintended ways in response to road safety initiatives, but the magnitude and consequences of these changes are controversial. It is hoped that this report will provide a basis for reasoned discussion of the issue, leading to some resolution, which will result in improvements in the safety benefits achieved by road safety programmes.

Controversy surrounding the discussion of behavioural adaptation has generally centred on the interpretation of what causes it, and how complete it is, not on whether it occurs. A number of researchers (e.g. 1, 2, 3, 4, 5, 6) have developed models of driver behaviour which, to some extent or another, explain a process similar to behavioural adaptation. Each of these models has something to contribute to our understanding of behavioural adaptation, and it is therefore not the purpose of the report to select one or another of the explanations as being the correct one. Rather, an overview of research, both empirical and theoretical, is presented. In this way, the report concentrates on developing an understanding of behavioural adaptation, rather than attempting to support one explanation for what has been observed.

I.4. HISTORICAL PERSPECTIVE

Summala (8) reports that early road safety programmes were based on a skills model of driving in which the driving task was viewed as a skill which needed to be developed, and failures in the system, (i.e., accidents) were the result of a failure to properly learn the required skills. More recent models of driver behaviour, and applied research, have addressed driving as a task with greater cognitive influence than was previously thought important. The driving task requires a great many decisions by the driver, and therefore factors which affect decision making also influence driving behaviour. Drivers with the greatest skills are not necessarily less likely to have accidents (9). The cognitive component of driving will be influenced, to a large extent, by the motivation of the driver.

Another characteristic of early engineering models (10) of driver behaviour was a tendency to view the driver as a non-responding component in the system (this view is still prevalent in some areas of road safety today). In such models it was assumed that a change in the driving environment, which was designed to improve safety, would lead to a change in driving behaviour, and the result would be the expected safety benefit. Drivers were not expected to change any behaviours other than those which the designer manipulated, or wanted to change. However, this simplistic view of the driver has been replaced with a more complex view in which drivers respond to changes in the road system and the vehicle in order to serve their needs, which may not be consistent with the goal of greater safety.

I.5. IMPLICATIONS FOR ROAD SAFETY

The importance of the topic will become evident in later chapters, which describe the studies in which behavioural adaptation has been observed. But it should be clear that, if drivers respond to safety measures in unanticipated ways, then the effectiveness of the safety measure, and the predictions of its benefits, may be reduced. It is, therefore, very important to understand when, why and how drivers will adapt their behaviour to changes made. An understanding of the adaptation and of the programme elements which result in complete adaptation, will allow road safety specialists to select those programmes and measures which will produce the greatest safety benefit for the entire road system.

The cost implications of failing to take behavioural adaptation into consideration are great. Major road improvement programmes can cost tens of millions of dollars and, if they do not produce the expected benefits, future funding for such programmes may be in doubt. If vehicle manufacturers are required to install new safety systems, and consumers are required to pay for them, there should be observable safety benefits, or such changes will be resisted with greater effort in the future.

One implication of attempting to study behavioural adaptation is that it becomes necessary to collect data on the behaviour of individual drivers. That is, accident and fatality data are not as useful because they cannot contribute to an understanding of the process of change which produced them. Accident and fatality data are only a summary, or final result of a series of changes which have taken place.

REFERENCES

1.   ADAMS, JGU. Risk and freedom: The record of road safety regulation. Transport Publishing Projects. Cardiff, 1985.

2.   COWNIE, AR and CALDERWOOD, HH. Feedback in accident control. Operation Research Quarterly, 17, 235-262. Baltimore, 1966.

3.   FULLER, R. A conceptualization of driving behaviour as threat avoidance. Ergonomics, 27, 1139-115. London, 1984.

4.   MOLEN, HH VAN DER and BOTTICHER, AMT. Risk models for traffic participants: a concerted effort for theoretical operationalizations. In ROTHENGATTER, JA and BRUIN, RA. Road users and Traffic safety. Assen, The Netherlands: Van Gorcum, 1987.

5.   NAATANEN, R and SUMMALA, H. A model for the role of motivational factors in drivers' decision making. Accident Analysis and Prevention, 6, 243-261. Oxford, 1974.

6.   WILDE, GJS. The theory of risk homeostasis: Implications for safety and health. Risk Analysis, 2, 209-225. New York, 1982.

7.   WILDE, GJS. Critical issues in risk homeostasis theory. Risk Analysis, 2, 249-258. New York, 1982.

8.   SUMMALA, H. Modelling driver behaviour. A pessimistic prediction? In L, EVANS and RC SCHWING, (eds), Human Behaviour and Traffic Safety (pp. 43-65). Plenum Press. New York, 1985.

9.   WILLIAMS, AF and O'NEILL, B. On-the-road driving records of licensed race drivers. Accident Analysis & Prevention, 6, 263-270. Oxford, 1974.

10.   EVANS, L. Human behaviour feedback and traffic safety. Human Factors, 27, 555-576. Santa Monica, 1985.

Chapter II

DEFINITION AND ISSUES

II.1. INTRODUCTION

Generally, reports prepared by the OECD Road Transport Research Programme provide state-of-the-art reviews and assessments of programmes and countermeasures developed to respond to priority needs and requirements of road safety authorities in Member countries. The topic of this report is somewhat different in that it deals with a more conceptual issue, one that was, prior to the report, not well defined, and one that has created a great deal of controversy amongst researchers. In fact, it is the goal of the report to assist the reader in developing an understanding of behavioural adaptation and its effect on road safety. It is anticipated that in five to ten years, an expert group will be able to return to the topic and find a great deal more research to discuss.

Behavioural adaptation is important to both road safety practitioners and researchers. Clarification of it should result in improvements in road safety programmes and in the research designed to evaluate them. In addition, many Member countries are concerned about the implications of theories like Risk Homeostasis (1, 2) for their road safety programmes because they have been used to argue against continued government promotion of road safety. It should be recognised that, in fact, Risk Homeostasis theory does not imply that all safety programmes will be ineffective. As a result of the conceptual nature of behavioural adaptation and the controversy associated with theories which suggest that drivers adapt to changes in the road system, it was decided that a chapter was needed to more thoroughly discuss the issues related to it.

In addition to presenting a discussion of the issues associated with behavioural adaptation, the chapter suggests a definition of the term and describes how behavioural adaptation is identified. Defining an abstract term like behavioural adaptation proved more difficult than anticipated. As a result, our definition may lack scientific rigour, and will be subject to criticism by those most interested in theory development and those who seek precise definitions. On the other hand, it was felt that the term needed to be defined in a manner which made its importance clear to both researchers and practitioners.

19

II.2.1.   Epistemologocal basis

Behavioural adaptation is neither a theory nor an hypothesis. Rather, it is a term which describes measurable behaviour changes, which are unintended, and which occur following a road safety programme (safety education, change to a vehicle, or modification to the road network). It is at the same level of abstraction as a concept in a theory, in that it cannot itself be operationalized, but specific instances of it can be operationalized. Therefore, it can be measured and studied as a dependent measure in road safety research, with the operational definition dependent on the exact context of the research. For example, one can consider the possibility of behavioural adaptation occurring in response to the introduction of studded tyres. Operationally, behavioural adaptation, in this case, might be defined as the observed increase in speed, or increased driving intensity under adverse conditions, or shorter headways on ice- and snow-covered roads. The operational definitions are applicable to the specific example, but the effects observed can be described as examples of behavioural adaptation.

Behavioural adaptation is not associated with any one particular theory of road user behaviour and as such it does not have the explanatory power of a theory. The mechanisms that have been proposed to explain behavioural adaptation are controversial, and it is not the purpose of the report to select one or another of these explanations. In fact, the report will provide a basis for discussing behavioural adaptation outside the context of any one theory. In this way it is hoped that the practical implications can be established, and that additional theoretical development can proceed in an open and positive environment.

Behavioural adaptation is not part of an existing theory, but it is not new, nor was the concept created by the authors of the report. The label for the concept was developed for the report in order to provide a descriptive term for a controversial concept. Behavioural adaptation has, however, become an important issue following the work of Wilde (1, 2), in which adaptation to changing situations in the road system was clearly outlined. Wilde proposed that the main reason for such changes is a phenomenon known as risk homeostasis. Wilde predicts that road users attempt to maintain a constant level of risk in their lives. However, this is only one explanation for behavioural adaptation, and other explanations including increased mobility, utility, and pleasure seeking have also been proposed as explanations.

II.2.2.   Retrospective analyses

Much of the research cited in the chapters which follow was not designed to investigate behavioural adaptation. With a few exceptions it has been necessary to use research which had other purposes, and to retrospectively analyse behavioural data in these reports to determine if there is evidence of behavioural adaptation. The problem of having to rely on retrospective analyses is not unique to the report, but is consistent with discussion of some of the models of road user behaviour which attempt to provide explanations for behavioural adaptation. The reason for the lack of prospective studies is that the concept has only recently been formalised and therefore no body of research has developed. It is anticipated that one function of the report will be to stimulate additional research into behavioural adaptation, research which will be prospective rather than retrospective.

II.2.3.   Accident and fatality data vs behavioural data

Fatality and accident rates have been used extensively to evaluate road safety programmes. The problem with these data is that they only provide a partial picture of what has happened as a result of a programme. If it is concluded that a programme is successful using accident and fatality data it must be assumed, in the case of a programme which required a behaviour change, that the behaviour did in fact change, and that the benefit did not occur as a result of some other system change. In the case of a programme which did not require road users to change their behaviour, such as a modification to the vehicle, it must be assumed that no unexpected behaviours changed, and that the safety benefit was due to the vehicle change only. It is very likely that in both cases such assumptions are not always tenable.

Assumptions must also be made if a programme is deemed to have failed following an evaluation conducted using accident and fatatlity data. That is, if these data indicated no change in the accident and fatality rate, it must be assumed that no change in behaviour occurred, or that the safety change was ineffective. These two assumptions may be incorrect and may result in the rejection of a programme which produced a desired behaviour change and was therefore successful in that respect, but the behaviour change did not result in the expected accident and fatality change. It may be that other behaviours also changed and that these additional changes were the cause of the programme failure.

For example, Jonah and Lawson (3) evaluated the effectiveness of seat belt legislation in Canadian provinces using both fatality and injury data and behavioural data. The injury and fatality data indicated that the seat belt wearing laws were only marginally effective, but looking at the behavioural data they found that the laws had substantially increased the wearing rate of seat belts. In this example, reliance on the accident and fatality statistics would have resulted in the rejection of seat belt laws as an effective road safety programme. However, the inclusion of behavioural data in their study demonstrated that the desired behaviour change had occurred, but that other factors were influencing the results. Rather than conclude that seat belts and seat belt legislation are ineffective, it is possible to conclude, using the behavioural data, that seat belts are being used, but that certain groups of drivers are more likely to be responsible for accidents. The basic countermeasure is successful, but its selective application reduced its effectiveness.

A number of researchers have considered drivers' responses to safety regulation by studying changes in fatality rates. Some of these studies have concluded that behavioural adaptation may have eliminated all the safety benefits created by the programmes they evaluated (1, 2, 4, 5, 6, 7). Others have argued that the safety benefits were not eliminated (8, 9, 10, 11, 12, 13). These studies are somewhat controversial because of the assumptions made, and because the variables selected for inclusion in the prediction equations can make substantial differences in the results obtained. In addition, there are many exogenous variables acting on the safety system which influence the effectiveness of safety programmes.

It may be possible to conclude from fatality and accident data that road users have adapted to road safety programmes. However, the conclusion is somewhat limited in its usefulness when it is impossible to confirm if the programme achieved its initial goal of a behaviour change, followed by adaptation, or if the programme simply failed. Employing behavioural adaptation to explain programme failure is inappropriate if behavioural data are not available. Therefore, the evaluation of programmes must include behavioural data which can demonstrate the process of behaviour change.

II.2.4.   Spatial and temporal manifestations

The definition of behavioural adaptation does not define a temporal or spatial range for behavioural adaptation. This is due, in part, to the fact that there is only very limited data on behavioural adaptation in the research literature. Ideally, it should be possible to specify both temporal and spatial parameters for behavioural adaptation or, if that is not possible, to provide spatial and temporal limitations for behavioural adaptation. If these limitations cannot be provided, then failure to find or demonstrate behavioural adaptation can be criticised by simply arguing that one did not search far enough or wait long enough for the adaptation to occur. If this type of argument can be invoked, then behavioural adaptation cannot be disproved, a necessary condition if it is to be scientifically acceptable.

Evans (14) has suggested that changes in behaviour will occur very quickly if road users are aware of the change which has been made. Thus, a change which is easily perceived by the road users will result in behavioural adaptation occurring very quickly, within hours, days or weeks. On the other hand, changes in the system such as improved traffic patterns may not be immediately detectable by the road user, and as a result a longer time span may be needed if the adaptation is to be identified. In this case, a time span of months or years may be needed for road users to become fully aware of the change and of how they can adapt it to their needs.

The inability to define temporal and spatial boundaries for the study of behavioural adaptation does not mean the concept is not useful. It is proposed that with sufficient research it will be possible to develop guidelines which can be used for the study of behavioural adaptation. The research reviewed in the following chapters will also provide the reader with an indication of how quickly drivers adjust their behaviour to various changes and of the types of changes which result in relatively slow adaptation.

II.2.5.   Adaptation to non-safety changes

Behavioural adaptation is not limited to changes in the transportation system which are intended to improve safety. Most of the theories place a heavy emphasis on the association between driver behaviour and safety. However, behavioural adaptation is concerned with how road users adapt to changes in the system, whether the changes were instituted for the purposes of safety or not.

The roadway engineer may design a new intersection to improve traffic flow. If the success of the change is monitored by means of the number of vehicles passing a certain point, it may be possible to conclude that a successful change has been made. If the number of vehicles moving through the intersection does not increase, it is not necessarily the case that the engineering change was ineffective. It may be that the engineering change was the right one, but that drivers adapted to that change, and the adaptation reduced the traffic flow. To correct the problem, it may be necessary to deal with the adaptation rather than attempt a totally new solution. By collecting data on how drivers change their behaviour in response to the intersection improvement, that is, by measuring speed through the area, number of stops, etc., greater information is available to describe how the change worked or failed to work. These additional data may assist in explaining why anticipated changes did not occur and will assist in determining what corrective action is needed.

II.3. BEHAVIOURAL ADAPTATION

II.3.1. Definition

The definition of behavioural adaptation presented below was developed in the context of road safety. The definition may be broadened to encompass other activities, but as the report focuses on road safety the definition reflects this orientation. Note that the definition does not provide any suggestion as to the motivating factors which might cause the adaptation to occur.

-- Behavioural adaptations are those behaviours which may occur following the introduction of changes to the road-vehicle-user system and which were not intended by the initiators of the change;

-- Behavioural adaptations occur as road users respond to changes in the road transport system such that their personal needs are achieved as a result, they create a continuum of effects ranging from a positive increase in safety to a decrease in safety.

II.3.2. Assumptions

For behavioural adaptation to occur, it must be assumed that there is feedback to road users, that they can perceive the feedback (but not necessarily consciously), that road users have the ability to change their behaviour, and that they have the motivation to change their behaviour. Feedback refers to knowledge and information received from the system (road-vehicle-road user) which results from changes in road users' behaviour. Feedback, in this sense, is a major component of a number of driver behaviour models (1, 2, 15, 16, 17, 18).

Evans (14) addresses the issue of behavioural adaptation by describing a number of studies in which there have been both negative and unanticipated positive benefits from modifications to the transport safety system. Evans proposes that feedback, the process by which road users find out about changes

23

in the system, is primarily responsible for the behaviour change which occurs following an initial response to the system. He presents the following formalization, which he argues represents the relationship between expected and actual safety benefits from changes to the transport system:

Actual change in = (1-f) Expected change in level of safety level of safety

"where f is a parameter that characterizes the degree to which there is feedback, or interactions, in the system." (14 p.558)

Feedback occurs at a number of different levels. There is immediate feedback which, for example, would involve the perception of a newly installed traffic sign. Next, there is feedback from the system components, the vehicle, the road, the driver and other road users. This feedback provides drivers with information about how their responses to the initial change is affecting vehicle performance and the behaviour of other road users, as well as how the initial change in behaviour is affecting personal goals.

In addition, there is more subtle feedback which results from observing the road system over time, and detecting changes in other drivers' behaviours and the occurrence of incidents in the transport system such as accidents and near-collisions. This latter form of feedback probably cannot be verbalized by the road user, and must be inferred from long-term changes in behaviour. This raises the issue of whether drivers must be aware of feedback for it to affect their behaviour. In other areas of psychology, it has been argued that people need not be aware of stimuli in order for them to have an effect on behaviour, so it is quite likely that the driver does not need to be aware of the subtle feedback, which may occur over a long period of time, for it to affect behaviour.

For behavioural adaptation to occur, we must also assume that drivers are able to change their behaviour in response to the feedback they receive. Wilson and Anderson (19) indicated that drivers were able to perceive a difference between cross-ply tyres and radial-ply tyres, but were unable to change their behaviour very much in response to the perceived differences. There was feedback from the tyres, and drivers perceived that the radial-ply tyres performed better than the cross-ply tyres, but they were unable to take advantage of the change because of limitations in their driving skills. In addition, drivers may be unable to take advantage of perceived improvements in road design or vehicle performance because of laws which control driving behaviour and limitations on other components in the system.

Finally, for behavioural adaptation to occur, there must be some motivation to change behaviour. If a safety feature is perceived to improve safety, and the driver enjoys the added safety benefit, then there is little motivation to change behaviour to take advantage of the system change. This is, in fact, what may happen with road safety education and publicity programmes discussed in Chapter V. If the programmes are successful they convince road users that a situation is dangerous and suggest a change to reduce the danger. If road users accept the suggested behaviour change, they must be accepting the premise of a dangerous situation. However, many road system changes make it possible for road users to impose their motivations on the system, thus allowing for decreased travel time, increased travel distance, maintenance of a constant level of risk, or some other motivation which is of greater relevance to the driver than the increased safety.

II.3.3.   Process

At what point following a system change does behavioural adaptation occur? When a change is made to one component of the road-vehicle-user system, road users may be required or may be expected to respond to the change in some way which is consistent with a goal of greater safety. Thus, a safety measure may elicit an initial response from the road user. The initial response may be predictable and lead to some safety benefit. However, the initial response to the change is not what we are concerned with in this report. Behavioural adaptation occurs after the initial response and is a process during which road users incorporate the change into their normal behaviour, modifying the initial response on the basis of their perceptions of the vehicle, the road, other road users and their personal goals of safety and mobility.

It is also possible that a change in the driving environment will not elicit an initial response, because no response is necessary for the safety benefit to occur. For example, when the interior of vehicles was modified to make them safer, drivers did not have to change their behaviour in order to take advantage of the change. Likewise, the first time drivers use radial tyres (rather than cross-ply tyres) or switch to studded snow tyres, they are not required to modify their behaviour in response to the change. Thus, in these cases no initial response is required or expected. In fact, if drivers did not change their behaviour, the full safety benefit of the change would be achieved.

However, other safety measures result in clearly definable initial responses which are predictable and sometimes required by law. For example, if drivers respond to mandatory seat belt laws by putting on a seat belt, then there is an obvious initial response. Likewise, if a stop sign is installed or modifications are made to more accurately convey the danger inherent in a curve, then drivers can be expected to stop in the former case and to respond by reducing their speed in the latter case.

To demonstrate behavioural adaptation we can return to the examples noted above. In the case of studded tyres (20) and radial tyres (19, 21) where no initial response was expected, it was shown that driving speeds were higher with the safer tyres (although the change in speed was not statistically significant for radial tyres). Behavioural adaptation need not eliminate all the safety benefit resulting from a change. Rumar et al (20) note that, although drivers drove faster with studded tyres, there remained a net safety gain.

In studies looking at modification to curve approaches (22) and stop signs (23), drivers changed their behaviour after the initial response. Behavioural adaptation in these cases took the form of increased speeds and alternative route selections. In the case of seat belt use laws (24, 25), no behavioural adaptation was detected, although it was argued [see discussion following (25)] that either the changes were too small to detect, the adaptive behaviours studied may not have been the best ones to investigate, or the adaptation might take a longer period of time to develop (one year was the time period for the latter study).

In these examples, the initial response was relatively easy to predict. However, in a study conducted by Ritchie (26), it was found that drivers reacted to curve warning signs by travelling faster around the corner than they did when there was no sign present. It may be argued in this case that the initial response of slowing down as a result of seeing a curve warning sign occurred in the past and that the need for a decrease in speed proved, over many trials, to be incorrect. As a result, when new curve warning signs are observed, there is no need for an initial response to each sign, and all that is observed is the behavioural adaptation. Ritchie suggests that the signs gave drivers greater confidence in their decision to drive at a particular speed around the curve.

REFERENCES

1. WILDE, GJS. The theory of risk homeostasis: Implications for safety and health. Risk Analysis. 2, 209-225. New York, 1982.

2. WILDE, GJS. Critical issues in risk homeostasis theory. Risk Analysis. 2, 249-258. New York, 1982.

3. JONAH, BA and LAWSON, JL. The effectiveness of the Canadian mandatory seat belt use laws. Accident Analysis and Prevention. 16, 433-450. Oxford, 1984.

4. ADAMS, JGU. Risk and freedom: The record of road safety regulation. Transport Publishing Projects. Cardiff, 1985.

5. ORR, LD. The effectiveness of automobile safety regulation: Evidence from the FARS data. American Journal of Public Health. 74, 1384-1389. Washington, 1984.

6. PELTZMAN, S. The effects of automobile safety regulation. Journal of Political Economy. 83, 677-725. Chicago, 1975.

7. WILDE, GJS. Notes on the interpretation of traffic accident data and of risk homeostasis theory: a reply to L. Evans. Risk Analysis. 6, 95-101. New York, 1986.

8. EVANS, L. Risk homeostasis theory and traffic accident data. Risk Analysis. 6, 81-94. New York, 1986.

9. EVANS, L. Comments on Wilde's notes on "risk homeostasis theory and traffic accident data". Risk Analysis. 6, 103-107. New York, 1986.

10. GRAHAM, JD. Technology, behaviour, and safety: An empirical study of automobile occupant-protection regulation. Policy Sciences. 17, 141-151. Amsterdam, 1984.

11. GRAHAM, JD and GARBER, S. Evaluating the effects of automobile safety regulation. Journal of Policy Analysis and Management. 3, 206-224. New York, 1984.

12.   GRAHAM, J and LEE, Y.   Behavioural response to safety regulation.
      Policy Sciences. 19, 253-273. Amsterdam, 1986.

13.   SHANNON, H.   Road-accident data: Interpreting the British experience
      with particular reference to the risk homeostasis theory. Ergonomics.
      29, 1005-1015. London, 1986.

14.   EVANS, L.   Human behaviour feedback and traffic safety. Human Factors.
      27, 555-576. Santa Monica, 1985.

15.   COWNIE, AR and CALDERWOOD, HH.   Feedback in accident control.
      Operational Research Quarterly. 17, 235-262. Elmsford, N.Y., 1966.

16.   FULLER, R.   A conceptualization of driving behaviour as threat
      avoidance. Ergonomics. 27, 1139-1155. London, 1984.

17.   NAATANEN, R and SUMMALA, H.   A model for the role of motivational
      factors in drivers' decision making.   Accident Analysis and
      Prevention. 6, 243-261. Oxford, 1974.

18.   MOLEN, HH VAN DER and BOTTICHER, AMT.   Risk models for traffic
      participants: a concerted effort for theoretical operationalizations.
      In JA Rothengatter and RA Bruin, Road Users and Traffic Safety. Van
      Gorcum. Assen, 1987.

19.   WILSON, W and ANDERSON, J.   The effects of tyre type on driving speed
      and presumed risk taking. Ergonomics. 23, 223-235. London, 1980.

20.   RUMAR, K, BERGGRUND, U, JERNBERG, P and YTTERBOM, U.   Driver reaction
      to a technical safety measure - studded tyres. Human Factors. 18,
      443-454. Santa Monica, 1976.

21.   BRINDLE, L and WILSON, W.   The effects of tyre type on driver
      perception and risk-taking.   Report No. C134/83.   Institute of
      Mechanical Engineers. London, 1983.

22.   SHINAR, D, ROCKWELL, T and MALECKI, J.   The effects of changes in
      driver perception on rural curve negotiation.   Ergonomics.   23,
      263-275. London, 1980.

23.   SMITH, RG and LOVEGROVE, A.   Danger compensation effects of stop signs
      at intersections. Accident Analysis and Prevention. 15, 95-104,
      Oxford, 1983.

24.   LUND, AK and ZADOR, P.   Mandatory belt use and driver risk taking. Risk
      Analysis. 4, 41-53. New York, 1984.

25.   O'NEIL, B, LUND, AK, ZADOR, P and ASHTON, S.   Mandatory belt use and
      driver risk taking: An empirical evaluation of the Risk-Compensation
      hypothesis. In L Evans and RC Schwing, (eds.), Human Behaviour and
      Traffic Safety (pp. 93-118). Plenum Press. New York, 1985.

26.   RITCHIE, M.   Choice of speed in driving through curves as a function of
      advisory speed and curve signs. Human Factors. 14, 533-538. Santa
      Monica, 1972.

Chapter III

HIGHWAY SAFETY

III.1. INTRODUCTION

The literature on highway safety improvements in OECD countries is vast and complex. The material which follows is not meant to be exhaustive, but rather representative of highway safety research in which behavioural adaptation can be identified. The effect of behavioural adaptation on safety is variable. It would have been desirable to include examples of behavioural adaptation to the road system by other road users such as pedestrians and cyclists, but these are not included for reasons of brevity. The studies presented are accepted by experts in the field as being of good methodological quality.

The following types of major road and environment safety improvement studies were selected for review: pavement lane widening, shoulder widening, centre line marking, edge line marking, lighting of urban arterials, lighting of freeways, and increasing intersection sight distance. All of these improvements are visible to the driver and exert direct influence on vehicular control. Furthermore, with the exception of intersection sight distance improvements, all of them impose a continuous influence over some period of driving time. That is, the driver is exposed to the change over several miles and is given some period of time to adapt to the improvement, thus giving behavioural adaptation effects full opportunity to be manifested.

The Chapter is organised with the accident and driver behaviour data for the seven types of improvements reviewed first. The implications of these findings relative to driver behaviour adaptation are discussed in a later section. Finally, the Chapter is concluded with some general observations pertaining to highway safety improvements and driver behaviour adaptation.

III.2. ROADWAY CROSS-SECTION

III.2.1. Lane width and accidents

Research studies in the United States have generally shown that accident rates decrease with an increase in the width of the traffic lane. The results of recent accident studies concerned with lane width for two-lane rural roads were summarised and indicate that as lane width increases, accidents per million vehicle-miles decreases (1).

29

More recently, accident studies concerning the safety effects of lane width were reviewed (2). After eliminating studies with major flaws, it was concluded that, in general qualitative terms, the accident rates of run-off-road (ROR) and opposite-direction (OD) type accidents decrease with increasing lane width. Other accident types, such as rear-end and angle accidents, are not directly affected by lane width.

To quantify the benefits and costs resulting from lane widening and other roadway and roadside improvements, detailed traffic, accident, and roadway data were collected on 4 951 miles of two-lane roads in seven states. Wider lanes was one of the factors found to be most related to reduced accidents. Based on a predictive model, the effects of lane width on related accidents were quantified as follows: the first foot of lane widening corresponds to a 12 per cent reduction in related accidents; two feet of widening (e.g. widening lanes from 9 to 11 feet) results in a 23 per cent reduction, three feet results in a 32 per cent reduction, and four feet of widening would result in a 40 per cent reduction. These reductions apply only for lane widths between 8 and 12 feet.

III.2.2. _Lane width and driver behaviour_

According to an analysis of free speeds measured in New South Wales on straight lengths of road on two-lane rural highways, an increase of pavement width increased the free speed (3). An increase in mean speed of 2 mph was found for each 1 ft increase in pavement width for cars as compared with 1.1 mph for trucks. This effect was based on pavement widths ranging from 18 to 24.5 ft.

Speeds of individual vehicles prior to and after a lane width reduction on a two-lane rural road were measured in another study (4). The roadway was basically level and straight with few no-passing zones. Speeds for both familiar and unfamiliar motorists, based on licence plate identification, were observed. Average vehicle speeds decreased after the lane reduction for both familiar and unfamiliar drivers by 2.9 mph and 4.2 mph, respectively. In addition, these investigators measured lane placement of individual vehicles prior to and after the lane width reduction. Lane placement distance was measured from the edge of the pavement to the centre of the nearest tyre tread path of the rear wheel. After the lane width reduction, vehicles travelled approximately 0.8-0.9 ft closer to the pavement edge.

Erratic manoeuvres have frequently been used as an indicator of unsafe traffic operations and as a surrogate measure for traffic accidents. Erratic manoeuvres prior to and after the lane width reduction were also measured. The number of observed erratic manoeuvres increased about 1.5 times after the lane reduction. No accidents were recorded during the data collection period 1974-1976. The erratic manoeuvre rate -- [(number of erratic manoeuvres x 1 000)/ADT] -- was 43.3. The types of erratic manoeuvres recorded were steering corrections (three observed), ran off road (seven observed), and crossed centre line (16 observed).

A study of the effects of various geometric and environmental factors, including lane width, on the speeds for two-lane rural highways was performed in Ontario, Canada (5). The effect of lane width was modelled with an exponential function. Lane width was treated as a linear factor with an ideal lane width of 4 m (13.1 ft). The coefficient of the lane width factor then determined the rate at which the speed would decrease for each metre by which lane width falls short of 4 m (13.1 ft).

For the practical range of lane widths from 3.3 to 3.8 m (10.8 ft to 12.5 ft) it was found that the operating speed of a given location is decreased by approximately 5.7 km (3.5 mph) for each metre of reduction in lane width. The coefficient of -5.67 and standard error of 2.31 indicate a reasonably high level of statistical significance. In accordance with the model developed, it was speculated that the speed reduction rate for lane widths less than 3.3 m (10.8 ft) would be even greater and that, for lane widths larger than 3.8 m (12.5 ft), this rate would be less. These authors conclude that the sensitivity of speed to lane width was 6 km/hr per m (1.1 mph per ft).

In summary, the studies reviewed over the past 30 years suggest a strong safety benefit associated with lane widening. Investigations in different countries consistently show a reduction in accidents with increases in pavement lane width. An examination of the effects of lane width on driver behaviour indicates that average vehicle velocities increase. Based on the studies reviewed, a reasonable estimate of the magnitude of the increase in speed seems to be on the order of 1-2 mph per foot of increased lane width. In addition, one of the reviewed studies suggested that lane width affects vehicle lateral placement and the incidence of erratic manoeuvres. The implications of these findings with regard to driver behaviour adaptation are discussed later.

III.2.3. Shoulder width and accidents

In the 1982 synthesis of safety research, it was reported that studies on the width of shoulders related to traffic accident rates have had mixed results (1). Early research had indicated that accidents increase with increasing shoulder width. In 1960, in Oregon, 346 miles of rural two-lane tangents (straight sections) were studied, and it was concluded that accident frequency increased with increasing shoulder widths for all volume ranges studied (6). More recent studies have generally shown that the accident rates have been reduced as shoulder widths increase.

It was reported that wider shoulders were associated with generally lower rates of single-vehicle accidents for three terrain conditions of flat, rolling, and mountainous (2). This analysis accounted for lane width, average daily traffic, average recovery distance and sideslope ratios. The accident rate in flat and rolling areas was noticeably higher for shoulder widths of zero or one foot than for the two- or three-foot category, but levelled off for shoulder widths greater than three feet. In mountainous terrain, four- or five-foot shoulders had a far lower mean rate than narrower shoulders, but the rate increased slightly for shoulders wider than six feet.

The effects of shoulder widening on related accidents were also determined by Zegeer et al (2) from their predictive model for paved and unpaved shoulders. For shoulder widths between 0 and 12 feet, the per cent reduction in related accidents due to adding paved shoulders was 16 per cent for two feet of widening; 29 per cent for four feet of widening, and 40 per cent for six feet of widening. Adding an unpaved shoulder would result in

13 per cent, 25 per cent, and 35 per cent reductions in related accidents for two, four and six feet of widening, respectively. These authors conclude paved shoulders are only slightly more effective than unpaved shoulders in reducing accidents.

III.2.4. Shoulder width and driver behaviour

In a review of the literature on vehicle speeds and shoulder design (7), the authors indicate that it is generally believed that increasing shoulder width or improving shoulder type will tend to increase the speed of vehicles on a road. An early study (8) did not support this proposition; however, two more recent studies do (3, 9). Leong 3) measured speeds at 31 sites on rural highways in New South Wales. The sites had varying lane and shoulder widths, and all sites had gravel shoulders. Only the speeds of isolated vehicles or those heading a platoon of vehicles were measured in the study. For shoulder widths between 0 and 6 feet it was found that an increase in mean speed of 0.32 mph occurred for each one foot increase in shoulder width for cars as compared with 1.35 mph for trucks.

Fambro et al (9) looked at vehicle speeds on three types of highway, for a variety of traffic volumes at 18 sites in Texas. The three types of roads were: a) two-lane highways without paved shoulders, b) two-lane highways with paved shoulders, and c) four-lane undivided highways without paved shoulders. Operational characteristics were recorded for more than 21 000 vehicles. They found speed differences between two-lane highways with and without paved shoulders at volumes greater than 250 vehicles/hr. Above this volume, paved shoulders appear to increase the average speed on the roadway by at least 10 per cent. The conversion of a full-width paved shoulder to an additional travel lane will increase the average speed by about 5 per cent on roadways carrying more than 150 vehicles per hour.

In a review of the literature on lateral placement and shoulder design (7), it was reported that one of the benefits of paved shoulders was that: "they improve (increase) the lateral separation between on-coming vehicles by increasing the effective width of main-line pavement" (10).

Taragin (8) recorded the results of a study which aimed to examine the relationship of lateral placement to shoulder type. He found that the lateral position of passenger cars moved progressively further from the centre line as the shoulders increased in width and improved in type. In other words, the clearances between meeting vehicles increased with increasing shoulder width and improved shoulder type.

A further study of the effect of shoulder design on vehicle lateral placement was carried out in Idaho (11). It was found that, on roads with 2.4 m (8 ft) shoulders, vehicles were placed approximately 0.8 m (2.6 ft) further from the centre line than on roads with 1.5 m (5 ft) shoulders. A reduction in shoulder width from 1.5 m (5 ft) to 1.2 m (4 ft) caused vehicles to move approximately 0.3 m (1 ft) nearer to the centre line. A further reduction of shoulder width to 0.9 m (3 ft) caused no further change in placement.

Average vehicle speeds, lane placement, and erratic manoeuvres prior to and after a shoulder width reduction on a two-lane rural road were measured in

Texas (4). Average vehicle speeds decreased by approximately 3.5 mph and vehicles travelled about 1 ft closer to the pavement edge after the shoulder width reduction. Two accidents were recorded during the data collection period 1974-1976. The erratic manoeuvre rate -- [(number of erratic manoeuvres x 1 000)/ADT] -- was 17.6. There was over a fourfold increase in observed erratic manoeuvres after the shoulder width reduction. The types of erratic manoeuvres recorded were encroachments (three observed), brake lights (one observed), and cross centre line (26 observed).

In summary, recent accident research on two-lane rural roads presents compelling evidence for an improved safety benefit associated with increased shoulder width. Moreover, the benefit can be very substantial, with accident reduction reaching as much as 40 per cent when 6 feet of paved shoulder is added to the roadway. Furthermore, the results from driver behaviour studies reviewed suggest that shoulder width has a definite impact on vehicle speeds, lateral placement and observed erratic manoeuvres. The more recent studies were very consistent in showing an increase in vehicle speeds with increases in shoulder width. Depending on other factors, speeds can be expected to increase by perhaps as much as 10 per cent when a paved shoulder is added to a two-lane rural highway. Studies of the effects of shoulder width on lane placement dating back to the 1950s show a consistent pattern of vehicles moving away from the centre line with increases in shoulder width. This is interpreted as being a significant benefit in that it has the effect of increasing the width of the pavement lane relative to the passing of opposing traffic. Consistent with this is the finding in one study that erratic manoeuvres, including centre line cross-overs, are less frequent when shoulders are present. Again, the implications of these findings with regard to driver behaviour adaptation are discussed later.

III.3. DELINEATION

III.3.1. Centre line markings and accidents

After a comprehensive literature review on the subject of roadway delineation, a recent Canadian study (12) stated that, in spite of the widespread use of centre lines, little quantitative data exist on its accident reduction effectiveness. They cite Glennon (13), who concluded as recently as 1979 that "no empirical data are available to show the safety effectiveness of centre lines on two-lane highways". Most of the accident studies on centre line markings are confounded by changing traffic volumes or geometric factors, making it virtually impossible to interpret the accident rate findings in any precise way. It is not surprising then that there are studies that indicate the centre line marking is associated with a decrease in accidents, no change in accidents, and an increase in accidents.

According to two reports (14, 15) on the U.S. FHWA Highway Marking Demonstration Project, highways with centre lines have significantly lower accident rates than those with no treatment at all, although it should be noted that not all of this reduction can be attributed to centre lining, as it may in part also be due to geometric and traffic factors. Other studies conducted in the states of Ohio and Minnesota reported reduced accident rates when centre lines are present (16).

Another study (17) found that comparison of before and after data indicated accidents increased on road sections which had been centre lined; however, these data could have been influenced by the large variability in year-to-year accident rates. It should also be noted that most of the locations striped were narrow pavements (19 ft or less in width), and this may be related to any increase reported.

On narrow roads the safety benefits of centre lining are open to question. Glennon (18) indicated that centre line striping on low-volume roads resulted in higher accident rates. His analysis indicated that centre lines applied to roads with less than 3.2 m (10 ft) lane widths and traffic volumes less than 1 000 vehicles per day appeared to increase accident rates. Germany (19) does not centre line roads of a width less than 5.5 m (approximately 18 ft) based on the theory that, in this situation, centre lining will increase the accident rate.

The Canadian review of centre line delineation studies (12) concludes:

"... test results have indicated no decrease, and actually increases, in accident rates on roads that have been centre lined. Some test data also indicate that centre lining is more effective on straight sections than horizontal or 'winding' roadway sections. Based on the limited data available, it is difficult to generalise, with any accuracy, the safety benefits of centre lining a two-lane road".

III.3.2. Centre line markings and driver behaviour

One study was reviewed which looked at the effects of various geometric and environmental factors, including centre line markings, on the speeds for two-lane rural highways in Ontario, Canada (5). Using a multiple linear regression model, they related measured speeds to the influencing properties of the highway and found no relationship between centre line marking and speed.

In summary, the review of studies of centre line markings and accidents produced inconsistent findings with regard to safety benefits. There are studies that show both positive and negative benefits associated with centre line markings on two-lane roads. Recent reviews in the U.S. and Canada both conclude that the safety effectiveness of centre lines is yet to be established. Only one study was reviewed on the driver behaviour effects of centre line markings, and it was unable to demonstrate an effect.

III.3.3. Edge line markings and accidents

A Canadian review of the literature on edge line studies (12) indicated that edge line markings significantly reduce accident rates (14, 15). A U.S. study indicated that the addition of edge lines to a roadway already centre lined would reduce the overall accident rate by 12 per cent (from 1.46 to 1.31 accidents per million vehicle-km). For tangent (straight) sections, the reduction rate was 14 per cent, while for winding sites a slight increase in the accident rate was noted.

Jackson (20) summarised accident reduction rates associated with the introduction of edge line markings at different locations. The median average accident reduction reported was 21 per cent. The study also indicates that the edge lining also reduces the severity of the accidents, as the fatal and injury-producing accident rates experienced greater reductions than overall accident rates. It should be noted that not all of the reductions reported by Jackson were statistically significant and that not all experiments have been as positive as those reported by Jackson. For example, a study in Buckinghamshire, England, indicated that there may be no benefits in the use of edge lines (21).

The analysis of the six State data (17) indicated that adding edge lines to roads that were already centre lined resulted in 12 per cent and 16 per cent decreases in night and fatal accident rates, while reductions of 22 per cent and 33 per cent were observed in the limited-visibility night fatal and injury accident rates.

III.3.4. Edge line markings and driver behaviour

In a rigorously controlled field study (22), the effects of nine delineation treatments including wide edge lines (150 mm), narrow edge lines (80 mm), and no edge lines on two-lane rural curve negotiation were compared. The tests were conducted at night with both sober and drinking drivers (BAC 0.05 per cent). The test subjects consisted of 36 males ranging in age from 25 to 56 years. Results of the analysis of the speed data indicated that the mean speed was slowest under the no edge line treatment. Under the no edge line treatment, the only pavement marking was an 80 mm wide centre line which was a white broken line with 3 m long stripes and 9 m long gaps. The 80 mm and 150 mm edge line treatments consisted of the centre line plus continuous edge lines newly painted with reflective white paint. The mean speeds for the wide edge lines, narrow edge lines and no edge lines were 67, 66 and 59 mph, respectively. The alcohol effects did not reach statistical significance, and the author concluded that alcohol did not affect the speed at which drivers chose to negotiate the track and therefore did not show the mean speeds for sober versus non-sober drivers. The author suggests that the higher mean speeds adopted by subjects under the edge line marking treatments are indicative of adaptive behaviour and reflects better driver performance:

"Since the speeds were still below those achieved during daytime, when the visual environment is at its richest, the increase in speed can be considered adaptive and an indication of increased confidence by the drivers in their judgements. The latter interpretation is also supported by the data derived from subjects ratings of their task."

In the same study (22), an analysis was conducted on lateral placement using as the dependent measure the frequency of lane departures. A lane departure was defined as an occasion when the right wheel of the vehicle was on or to the right of the centre line or the left wheel was on or to the left of the pavement edge. These occasions were counted throughout curve negotiation. The alcohol effects were significant in that there was an average of 3.7 lane departures for drivers with a BAC of 0.05 per cent compared with 2.3 for drivers with a placebo alcohol dose. The delineation main effects were not statistically significant, and there were no significant interactions for the frequency of lane departures measure. The author concludes that alcohol results in more extreme lateral placement and that this behaviour is non-adaptive in that it is so extreme that lane departures occur more frequently.

A driving simulator was used (23) to evaluate edge line treatments as well as other types of curve delineation conditions. Three edge line treatments were tested: a) no edge line; b) 4-inch edge line, and c) 8-inch edge line. Twelve male subjects (21 to 44 years of age) drove the simulator for two hours. A monetary incentive/penalty reinforcement schedule was used to maintain interest. Alcohol and task demand were also used as independent variables.

The results (23) indicated that edge line presence improved tracking behaviour in both the approach and negotiation of curves, and increased overall simulator performance, as reflected in increased monetary reward. Wide edge lines (8-inch) in comparison with narrow edge lines (4-inch) were associated with incremental performance benefits of between 1 and 11 per cent, although they were not statistically significant. Edge line presence was also associated with increases in curve entry speed and lateral acceleration in curve negotiation, which in the context of the observed tracking improvements were interpreted as evidence of increased driver certainty. According to the authors,

"... it must be concluded that edge line presence increased overall speed (decreased time), speed in the approach to curves, and lateral acceleration in curve negotiation, without adversely affecting tracking accuracy in the curve nor overall safety". (23).

In summary, the thrust of the evidence seems to suggest that the presence of edge lines on two-lane rural roads does produce a safety benefit. The picture is not totally consistent in that there are also studies of edge lines versus no edge lines that show no significant differences in the accident data. A rigorously controlled Australian field study and a U.S. driving simulator study examined the effects of edge line treatments on the driving behaviour of sober and non-sober test subjects (22, 23). In both studies edge line presence was associated with increased speeds. The effects of edge line treatments on tracking performance as measured by frequency of lane departures were not significant in the controlled field study. However, tracking performance in terms of lane placement improved with the presence of edge lines in the simulator study.

III.4. ROADWAY LIGHTING

III.4.1. Urban arterials

a) Lighting and accidents

An extensive literature review (24) identified research results relating roadway lighting to traffic safety and concluded that night accidents can be substantially reduced in number and severity by the use of good road lighting. A number of studies using before-and-after data with daylight accidents as a control have shown a reduction in night accidents with improved lighting systems on urban roadways.

Night-daylight accident ratios were investigated (25) for 105 miles of urban arterial roadway in Syracuse, N.Y., having various lighting levels. It was concluded that, because streets with little or no lighting had substantially higher night-daylight accident ratios, inadequate lighting contributes to accident hazards. A report (26) provides a summary of a study by Duff (27) giving results from six countries. While details of the studies are not known, they all appear to give percentage reductions which are reasonably consistent.

The effects of reduced lighting on 2 1/2 miles of a major arterial in Clearwater, Florida, were studied (28). Lighting was reduced from 1.8 HFC to 0.9 HFC (horizontal foot candles) by turning off alternate luminaires. The number of daylight accidents increased 3.7 per cent while the night accidents increased 39.5 per cent. These changes were significant at the 0.05 level.

Turner (29), (as reported in 26) studied ten sections of arterial roads in Sydney, Australia. Lighting on 130 miles of road varied from average levels of 1 700 to 12 500 lumens per 100 ft of roadway. During the three-year study, there was a 20 to 30 per cent reduction in night accidents due to improved lighting. As the amount of lighting which reached the road was increased, the ratio of night to daylight accidents decreased.

In another study, measurements of the existing lighting conditions for 100 sites on 30 mph roads mostly in "built-up" areas were made (30). The lighting variables measured were correlated to the daylight/night accident ratios for the same sites. The strongest relationship found was for average road surface luminance. An estimated increase of one candela per square metre was associated with a 35 per cent lower accident ratio. This relationship only applied to the range of conditions observed -- average road luminances in the range 0.5 to 2.0 candelas per square metre.

In 1977, based on a literature review on the effects of roadway lighting, it was reported: "No data (other than accident data) was found that reflects the effect of lighting on other aspects of traffic operations on arterial streets and only limited data is available that relates lighting to any type of traffic operational data on other types of roadways" (26). Based on the results of a recent international literature search, this statement seems to still be true today.

In summary, the preponderance of the evidence on the effects of roadway lighting on nighttime accidents on urban arterial streets suggests that substantial benefits are associated with improved lighting. Studies from several
countries consistently show the safety benefits of arterial street lighting. The reported reductions in accidents with improved lighting range from 20 to 57 per cent, depending on the conditions. No data were found on the effects of arterial lighting on driver behaviour.

III.4.2. Freeways

a) Lighting and accidents

The results of eliminating lighting on one side of three sections of Texas Interstate Highway I-35, with average daily traffic volumes of 22 000 to 53 000 vehicles per day, were analysed (31). Reductions in roadway lighting significantly increased the frequency, rate, and severity of night accidents. Night accidents on the unlit side increased by 47.1 per cent while accidents on the lighted side and in daylight all decreased. The results are statistically significant. The most significant increases were for night rear-end and pedestrian related accidents. Highway lighting reduction was found not to be a satisfactory energy saving measure due to the increase in accidents.

A report was made (32) on an extensive study of the effects of a 50 per cent reduction in continuous lighting on a 8.57 mile section of eight- to ten-lane freeway in Virginia (I-395). Lighting reduced the night accident rate by 44 per cent in the December to February period, and by 10 per cent in the March to May period (not statistically reliable). Accident data for the winter months (December to February), when heavy traffic volumes occur during the early hours of darkness, indicate that lighting was particularly effective.

A study looking at the effect of introducing lighting at interchanges over a ten-year study period (33) indicated no change in daylight accidents (83 to 80), but a substantial change in night accidents, dropping from 76 before lighting was installed to 43 after lighting was put in place.

Many researchers report (e.g. 33) that factors other than lighting were found to be more significant in their influence on freeway accidents. These include traffic volume, type of interchange, and degree of roadside development. Because traffic volume has such a dominant effect and can fluctuate widely during study periods, it is difficult to partial out this effect in most studies on freeway lighting. This notion was perhaps best expressed in the following: "With all of the sources of variation found in accident data, it is unlikely an unequivocal relationship can be developed between road lighting design parameters and accidents alone" (24).

b) Lighting and driver behaviour

The effects of freeway illumination on driving performance were studied (34) using 10 male and female subjects ranging in age from 28 to 58 who drove an instrumented vehicle over an illuminated section of the Connecticut Turnpike. Velocity under "free flow" conditions was measured under two nighttime illumination levels: 0.62 fc (normal lighting) and 0.22 fc (reduced lighting). It was reported that, under the higher illumination level, test subjects elected slightly higher speeds with significantly greater velocity variability than they did under the lower illumination level.

In another study, traffic observations were made under two intensities of artificial illumination, 0.2 fc and 0.6 fc and under daylight conditions over a five year period (35). Study sites included tangent, curve, on-ramp and off-ramp and control sites for the first two types of sites. Statistically significant changes in mean velocity were obtained in all but one of the eight possible lanes for passenger vehicles at the curve and off-ramp when the illumination intensity was changed. Changes in velocity at the tangent and on-ramp sites were not as great as at the other two sites, but all mean velocity changes were less than 2 mph, even when statistically significant. Those changes that did take place indicate a tendency for mean speed to decrease with an increase in lighting intensity. Similar changes were found for mean velocities of commercial vehicles, but were not statistically significant, because of smaller sample sizes.

The effectiveness of partial interchange lighting (PIL) versus complete interchange lighting (CIL) was investigated (36). Partial lighting was defined as lighting that consists of a few luminaires (1-4) located in the general areas of freeway entrance and exit ramps. For the exit ramp, all the study conditions (CIL, PIL, no lighting, and daylight) had average velocities that were almost identical. Differences between study conditions were never more than a few feet per second, and these were not consistent (i.e. the plots crossed rather than remaining distinctly apart). For the entrance ramp, the velocity profiles were identical through the first 400 ft of the ramp (+1 ft/s) and then began to differ slightly at the merge point, with the velocities for the PIL conditions somewhat higher than the CIL, no lighting, and daylight conditions. The key dependent measure that led the authors to recommend CIL over PIL was frequency of brake activations. This measure, which they reasoned is dependent on the visual quality in the interchange area and is directly related to both the safety and the smoothness of traffic flow, showed a significant increase as the lighting was reduced from CIL to PIL. In addition, the location of the brake activations was negatively shifted when the lighting was reduced from CIL to PIL.

In summary the weight of the evidence seems to indicate that freeway lighting does produce a net gain in reducing nighttime accidents. To be sure, there are some contradictory and inconsistent findings, but the collective trend of all the studies is in the direction of a net benefit. The percentage reduction in nighttime accidents associated with improved lighting has been reported as high as 56 per cent. Only minimal changes in driver behaviour have been observed to be affected by freeway lighting. An instrumented vehicle study showed significantly greater velocity variability under higher illumination levels. And, statistically significant but small decreases (about 2 mph) in average vehicle velocity were observed in a traffic study with an increase in lighting intensity. It should be noted, however, that in both these studies the magnitude of the change in lighting intensity was small (0.22 fc to 0.62 fc). In another study, frequency of brake activations was reported to increase under reduced lighting conditions, which was interpreted to be a negative indication in terms of the quality of traffic operations.

III.5. INTERSECTION DESIGN

III.5.1. Intersection sight distance and accidents

A review of accident rates at intersections with problem sight obstructions indicated that the accident rate will generally decline if the sight obstructions are removed (37). For example, a before and after study (38) conducted in Concord, California, showed a decline in total accidents from 39 in the year before, to 13 in the year after, sight obstructions were removed, a 67 per cent reduction. In the same study, many other intersections at other locations in Concord were improved by use of signal installation or modification, delineation striping, improved pavement markings, and increased police enforcement. Although all improvements resulted in a reduction in accidents, the greatest percentage of reduction was experienced at the intersections where the sight distances were improved. It was estimated (39) that intersection accident potential could be reduced 10 to

25 per cent if visibility of an object on a cross road, as seen by a driver from a main-road vehicle 50 ft from the intersection, could be increased from a point 20 ft from the intersection to one 50 ft away.

The effect of poor sight distance and severe grade on accident occurrence was analysed in a study of intersection accidents in rural Virginia municipalities (40). The accident rate (per million vehicles) at intersections with severe grades was unexpectedly low (.97) as compared with an average rate of 1.13 for all intersections. Apparently drivers were aware of poor physical conditions and exercised more than average caution at those locations. On the other hand the high rate of accidents at places with restricted sight distances (1.33) was due to the large number of angle collisions, a result of the inability of drivers to properly view vehicles approaching on cross streets.

In Australia a study was carried out on the approach speeds to low volume cross intersections whose vision was obstructed by a right sight restriction at the intersection (41). This study concentrated on drivers who were on the road carrying the greater volume but where the legal priority was governed by the give-way-to-the-right rule. The intention of this rule in Victoria is that a driver, on approaching such an intersection which is clear, should decelerate (and prepare to yield) until such a distance from the intersection that his vehicle could clear it without forcing an approaching vehicle, just out of sight on the right, to take evasive action. It showed that many drivers on the major road approached certain intersections of this type at a speed that would not have allowed them to stop their vehicle and avoid a potentially conflicting vehicle just out of sight on the right. It was also pointed out that this type of intersection sustains a high incidence of accidents.

Another study dealt with the approach speeds at intersections where there was a low and high probability of vehicles entering the road from the sight-restricted right cross road (42). The free approach speeds of vehicles whose drivers had prior exposure to the intersections were measured. An approach speed was not recorded if a driver could see moving vehicles on or near the intersection as he approached it. At the intersection with high-probability of cross traffic, the mean free approach speed was low. On the other hand, drivers approached the intersection with low-probability of cross traffic at higher speeds. Considering the large difference between the mean speeds at the two intersections and the relatively low speed variances within each situation, it was concluded that the expected frequency of vehicles from the right was a significant determinant of approach speeds, and that a large percentage of motorists determined their approach speeds incorrectly.

In summary, accident studies suggest that intersection sight distance improvements have a significant safety gain. Some accident reductions have been reported to be as high as 67 per cent where sight obstructions have been removed at intersections. Only one study was reviewed that was concerned with intersection sight distance and driver behaviour. Drivers in Australia were observed to approach sight restricted intersections at approach speeds based on their estimations of the probability vehicles would be entering the road.

III.6. HIGHWAY SAFETY IMPROVEMENTS AND DRIVER BEHAVIOUR ADAPTATION

Table III.1 summarises the overall safety effects and the influence of driver behaviour adaptation on the seven safety improvements reviewed in this analysis. As can be seen in Table III.1, it is suggested that there is a strong positive safety effect associated with four of the seven roadway safety improvements: increase in lane width, increase in shoulder width, arterial lighting, and increased intersection sight distance. Two roadway safety measures were rated as having a positive safety effect: edge line markings and freeway lighting. Centre line markings were given a mixed rating of negative and positive safety effects.

Table III.1 also summarises the status of the evidence concerning how driver behavioural adaptation influences the safety effects of the seven roadway improvements. The direction of this influence, whether negative or positive, is also presented. Increases in vehicle velocity were considered negative effects whereas decreased erratic manoeuvres, improved lane placement, and decreased braking frequency were rated as positive. There is enough evidence to suggest that the influence of driver behavioural adaptation is proven to exist for three of the safety improvements: increase in lane width, increase in shoulder width, and edge line markings. The direction of the driver behavioural adaptation effect is both negative and positive, depending on the behavioural measure used, for all three of these safety improvements. The evidence is non-existent or inadequate to establish any driver behavioural adaptation effects for centre line markings or arterial lighting. There is a very limited amount of data in the literature that suggests that a small driver behaviour adaptation influence might exist and affect freeway lighting and increase intersection sight distance improvements. The direction of the driver behavioural adaptation effect is probably slightly positive for freeway lighting, but possibly negative for increased intersection sight distance.

III.6.1. Lane width and shoulder width

Lane width and shoulder width safety improvements show similar results with regard to the safety effects and in terms of the influence of driver behavioural adaptation. Both show strong evidence for a substantial reduction in accidents when lane and shoulder widths are widened. Similarly, vehicle velocities increase, and there is some data that suggests that the number of observed erratic manoeuvres decreases with both of these improvements. It can be argued that the mechanism for the driver behavioural adaptation influence relative to lane and shoulder safety improvements involves driver perception of risk. With wider pavement lanes and shoulders, the driver perceives less risk or danger and therefore drives faster. Driving faster can be interpreted as a negative driver behavioural adaptation effect. However, in spite of this, the evidence suggests there is a substantial net safety benefit associated with wide pavement lanes and shoulders.

III.6.2. Centre line markings

The results of the analysis of the literature on centre line markings was surprising in that there were very mixed findings with regard to their safety benefits and little international literature was found on driver behaviour effects. It can be argued that the presence of centre line markings provides the driver with an important cue as to his/her proper position on the roadway relative to opposing traffic. It is an important reference for the second by second tracking of the roadway lane. Without the centre line, the task of tracking is more difficult and requires more perceptual and cognitive effort in performing directional control of the vehicle. The addition of the centre line does not actually increase the physical safety margin in terms of tracking error. However, the presence of the centre line does lessen the work-load of the tracking task, particularly during inclement weather. This line of reasoning would also suggest that the centre line markings should be most effective on "winding roadway" sections where the demand of the tracking task is the highest. Surprisingly, the accident data do not bear this out. Is behavioural adaptation operating here in that some drivers operate at too high speeds which are inappropriate for conditions when roads are enhanced with centre line markings? The one study reviewed on the relationship between centre line markings and vehicle speeds showed statistically insignificant results. An alternative explanation is that the driver attends less to the tracking task when the centre line is present even though there is no actual increase in the physical safety margin. Attention thus diverted from the steering task could possibly increase the likelihood of run-off-the-road accidents. Further research is needed to resolve this issue.

Table III.1.

SAFETY EFFECT, INFLUENCE AND DIRECTION OF BEHAVIOURAL ADAPTATIONS

Safety Measure	Safety Effect Behavioural	Influence of Behavioural Adaptation	Direction of Adaptation Effect
Increase in lane width	Strong positive	Proven	Positive & negative
Increase in shoulder width	Strong positive	Proven	Positive & negative
Centre markings	Negative & positive	Not proven	
Edge line markings	Positive	Proven	Positive & negative
Arterial lighting	Strong positive	Not Proven	--
Freeway lighting	Positive	Suggested	Possibly positive
Increased intersection sight distance	Strong positive	Suggested	Possibly negative

42

III.6.3. Edge line markings

The literature on edge line markings presents a much different picture
than that of centre line markings. There seems to be a positive safety
benefit associated with edge lines, although not as strong as shown for wider
pavement lanes and shoulders. There is also more data on the effects of edge
lines on driver behaviour, perhaps because of recent concerns about the
drinking-driver problem. Vehicle velocities do increase with the presence of
edge lines. However, vehicle placement in the pavement lane improves with
edge line treatments. Like centre line markings, edge lines do not actually
improve the physical margin of safety, but merely improve the driver's
perception of the physical limits of the roadway. In contrast with centre
lines, however, edge lines show a net gain in safety benefits.

III.6.4. Urban arterial lighting

The preponderance of the evidence on the effects of urban arterial
lighting on nighttime accidents suggests strong positive benefits are
associated with improved lighting. No data were available for this analysis
on the effects of improved arterial lighting on driver behaviour. From the
perspective of behavioural adaptation, it is conceivable that improved
arterial lighting could result in some forms of driver behaviour (e.g.
increased speeds) that could reduce its potential safety benefits. However,
research is required to answer this question.

III.6.5. Freeway lighting

Improved freeway lighting showed a positive safety benefit. The
benefit was not as strong in comparison with arterial lighting, but
nevertheless the balance of the evidence was in the direction of a net gain in
safety. Analysis of the limited literature available indicated that driver
behavioural adaptation effects seemed to be present with lighting changes but
they were of minor consequence.

III.6.6. Intersection sight distance

The accident studies showed a strong positive safety benefit from
intersection sight distance improvements. The driver behaviour data were
limited, but did seem to suggest that drivers do compensate in their approach
velocities to sight-restricted intersections. The lower accident rates at
intersections with physical grade problems in comparison with other
intersections suggest that drivers do adapt their behaviour. Unfortunately,
they may be taking greater risks.

III.7.   DISCUSSION

Studies of highway safety benefits associated with pavement width,
shoulder width, centre line markings, edge line markings, urban arterial
lighting, freeway lighting, and intersection sight distance were reviewed from

the perspective of driver behavioural adaptation. Changes to these features designed to increase safety are immediately discernible by the driver and therefore could be expected to elicit some form of behavioural adaptation relatively quickly.

The question remains whether there is some benefit to be gained by pursuing further behavioural adaptation questions with regard to any of the seven types of safety improvements. In comparison with accident studies, it is clear there is a lack of driver behaviour data available in the literature for most of the safety improvements reviewed. For example, very little was found in the way of behaviour adaptation data relative to improvements pertaining to intersection sight distance, arterial lighting, and pavement markings. Research is needed to clarify the relationships between specific safety improvements involving changes on the roadway and driver behaviour adaptation. One could argue that a better understanding of behavioural adaptation associated with any of these improvements could lead to greater benefits.

It may be that driver perception of risk is an important element in the mechanism governing driver behaviour adaptation. For example, vehicle velocities have been shown to be related to driver risk perception such that when perceived risk is low, drivers speed up and vice-versa (43). An increase in vehicle velocity is not always detrimental to highway safety; it is, however, if it is at the wrong time and place. Risk perception may be a key element in determining whether driver behaviour adaptation has a positive or negative influence on highway safety. More research is needed to fully understand how driver risk perception is mediated by roadway elements so that more can be done to keep driver adaptation a positive rather than a negative influence on safety improvements.

Of the seven improvements, it appears based on the accident and driver behaviour data cited above, that centre line and edge line markings warrant further investigation from the perspective of driver behavioural adaptation. In comparison to the other five types of safety improvements, the pavement marking accident data are equivocal in demonstrating a substantial net safety gain. This is particularly true for centre line markings on winding two-lane rural roads. In contrast to lane and shoulder widening improvements, pavement markings do not actually increase the physical safety margin of the roadway. Widening of the roadway provides more space for manoeuverability and can thus better accommodate driver errors. On the other hand, pavement markings increase the visibility of the roadway, without change in physical space to allow for increases in driver speed. This may produce conditions where the benefits of pavement markings, if not nullified, are at least partly reduced.

Irrespective of the nature of driver behaviour adaptation, there is no question that certain road safety improvements substantially reduce accidents. One of the best examples comes from Japan where road accident reduction in the 1970s was drastic (44). The worst record of road traffic deaths in Japan was 16 765, which occurred in 1970. This number decreased thereafter for nine years until 1979 when this number was reduced to 8 466. This number was almost half of the peak, despite the fact the number of motor vehicles had doubled and the total distance travelled by all vehicles increased by 1.7 times. During this time the government increased its expenditure for improving roads and related facilities from less than Yen 100 billion to over

Yen 800 billion. Koshi states, "It is commonly agreed that improvements and additions to road safety facilities have been the most effective factor for the dramatic reduction of road accidents in the 1970s".

REFERENCES

1.   BISSELL, HH, PILKINGTON, GB, MASON, JM and WOODS, DL. Chapter 1 -- Roadway cross section and alinement. In "Synthesis of safety research related to traffic control and roadway elements", Vol. 1, Report No. FHWA-TS-82-232. Federal Highway Administration. Washington, DC, 1982.

2.   ZEGEER, CV, HUMMER, J, REINFURT, D, HERF, L and HUNTER, W. Safety effects of cross-section design for two-lane roads, Vol. I. Final Report. Report No. FHWA-RD-87/008. Federal Highway Administration. Washington, DC, 1987.

3.   LEONG, HJW. Distribution and trend of free speeds on two-lane, two-way rural highway in New South Wales. Proc. ARRB 4, Part 1, 791-814. Nunawading, Victoria, 1968.

4.   MESSER, CJ, MOUNCE, JM and BRACKETT, RQ. Highway geometric design consistency related to driver expectancy. Vol. II, Research Report, FHWA, Report No. RD-81-036. Washington, DC, 1981.

5.   YAGAR, S and VAN AERDE, M. Geometric and environmental effects on speeds of two-lane highways. Transpn. Res. - A Vol. 17A, No. 4, pp. 315-325. Oxford, England, 1983.

6.   BLENSLEY, RC and HEAD, JA. Statistical determination of effect of paved shoulder width on traffic accident frequency. Highway Research Board Bulletin 240. Highway Research Board. Washington, DC, 1960.

7.   ARMOUR, M and MCLEAN, JR. The effects of shoulder width and type on rural traffic safety and operations. Australian Road Research, 13(4). Nunawading, Victoria, December 1983.

8.   TARAGIN, A. Driver behaviour as related to shoulder type and width on two-lane highways. Highway Research Board Bulletin, 170, pp. 54-76. Washington, DC, 1958.

9.   FAMBRO, DB, TURNER, DS and ROGNESS, RO. Operational and safety effects of driving on paved shoulders in Texas. Texas State Department Highways and Public Transportation and Federal Highway Administration. Rep. FHWA-TX-81/31+265-2F. FHWA. Washington, DC, 1981.

10.   PORTIGO, JM. State-of-the-art review of paved shoulders. Transport. Research Rec. 594, pp. 57-64. Washington, DC, 1976.

11.   JOROL, NH. Lateral vehicle placement as affected by shoulder design on rural Idaho highways. Proc. Highway Research Board 41, pp. 415-432. Washington, DC 1962.

12.   TRANSPORT CANADA, ROAD SAFETY AND MOTOR VEHICLE REGULATION DIRECTORATE.
       Cost-effectiveness of roadway delineation as a counter measure for
       accidents involving impaired drivers. Project 1264-27. Transport
       Canada. Ottawa, October 1985.

13.   GLENNON, JC. Design and traffic control guidelines for low volume
       rural roads. National Co-operative Highway Research Programme Report
       214. Transportation Research Board, National Research Council.
       Washington, DC, October 1979.

14.   BALI, SG, MCGEE, HW, TAYLOR, JI. State-of-the-art on roadway
       delineation systems. Science Applications Inc. El Segundo,
       California. Prepared for FHWA. Washington, DC, May 1976.

15.   BALI, SG, POTTS, R, FEE, JA, TAYLOR, JI, GLENNON, J. Cost effectiveness
       and safety of alternative roadway delineation treatments for rural
       two-lane highway. Vol. II, Final Report prepared for FHWA.
       Washington, DC, April 1978.

16.   US DEPARTMENT OF TRANSPORTATION, OFFICE OF HIGHWAY SAFETY. The 1982
       highway safety stewardship report. FHWA. Washington, DC, April 1982.

17.   US DEPARTMENT OF TRANSPORTATION. Office of Highway Safety, Federal
       Highway Administration. The 1982 highway safety stewardship report.
       Washington, DC, April 1981.

18.   GLENNON, JC. Accident effects of centerline markings on low-volume
       roads. January 1985. Paper prepared for presentation at 64th Annual
       Meeting Transportation Research Board. TRB. Washington, DC, 1985.19.

19.   DOMHAN, M. Pavement delineation technology in the Federal Republic of
       Germany. Federal Highway Research Institute. Cologne, 1981. Paper
       prepared for Durable pavement Markings Materials Workshop. Denver,
       1981.

20.   JACKSON, J. Reflections on keeping death off the road. Surveyor
       Magazine. Vol. 161, No. 4736. Manchester, April 1983.

21.   BUCKINGHAMSHIRE COUNTY COUNCIL. Road safety statistics and traffic
       flow, 1982. Section B, Report on an Edgeline Experiment. County
       Engineers Department. Buckingham, May 1982.

22.   JOHNSTON, IR. The effects of roadway delineation on curve negotiation
       by both sober and drinking drivers. Research Report ARR 128.
       Australian Road Research Board. Nunawading, Victoria, 1983.

23.   RANNEY, TA and GAWRON, VJ. Identification and testing of
       countermeasures for specific alcohol accident types and problems. Vol.
       II. General driver alcohol problem. National Highway Traffic Safety
       Administration/Federal Highway Administration, Report No. DOT-HS
       806-650. NHTSA. Washington, DC, December 1984.

24.   SCHWAB, RN, WALTON, NE, MOUNCE, JM and ROSENBAUM, MJ. Chapter 12 --
       Roadway lighting, in synthesis of safety research related to traffic
       control and roadway elements. Vol. 2. Report No. FHWA-TS-82-233.
       FHWA. Washington, DC, 1982.

25. BOX, PC. Comparison of accidents and illumination. Highway Research Record 416. Highway Research Board. Washington, DC, 1972.

26. JANOFF, MS, KOTH, B, MCCUNNEY, W, FREEDMAN, M, DUERK, C and BERKOVITZ, M. Effectiveness of highway arterial lighting. Report No. FHWA-RD-77-37. FHWA. Washington, DC, 1977.

27. DUFF, JT. Road lighting and the role of central government. Lighting Research and Technology, 6(4). London, 1974.

28. BOX, PC. Effect of lighting reduction on an urban major route. Traffic Engineering, Vol. 46, No. 10. Washington, DC, October 1976.

29. TURNER, JJ. The influence of road lighting on traffic safety and service. Australian Road Research Board Proceeding, Vol. 1. ARRB. Nunawading, 1962.

30. SCOTT, PP. The relationship between road lighting quality and accident frequency. Report No. LR929. Transport and Road Research Laboratory. Crowthorne, 1980.

31. RICHARDS, SH. The effects of reducing continuous roadway lighting to conserve energy -- a case study. Safe Journal, Vol. 9, No. 1. Newhall, California, 1979.

32. HILTON, MH. The effectiveness of freeway lighting in reducing accidents. Compendium of Technical Papers: ITE 49th Annual Meeting. Institute of Transportation Engineers. Washington, DC, 1979.

33. GRAMZA, K, HALL, JA and SAMPSON, W. Effectiveness of freeway lighting. Report No. FHWA-RD-79-77. FHWA. Washington, DC, February 1980.

34. ROCKWELL, TH and LINDSAY, GF. Driving performance, Part II. In Effects of illumination on operating characteristics of freeways. NCHRP Report No. 60, pp. 51-71. Highway Research Board. Washington, DC, 1968.

35. HUBER, MJ and TRACEY, JL. Effects of illumination on operating characteristics of freeways. NCHRP Report No. 60. Washington, DC, 1968.

36. JANOFF, MS, FREEDMAN, M and DECINA, LE. Partial lighting of interchanges. NCHRP Report No. 256. Washington, DC, 1982.

37. HAGENAUER, GF, UPCHURCH, J, WARREN, D and ROSENBAUM, MJ. Chapter 5 -- Intersections. In: Synthesis of safety research related to traffic control and roadway elements, Vol. 1, Report No. FHWA-TS-82-232. FHWA. Washington, DC, 1982.

38. MITCHELL, R. Identifying and improving high accident locations. Public Works. New York, December 1972.

39. DAVID, NA and NORMAN, JR. Motor vehicle accidents in relation to geometric and traffic features of highway intersections, Vol. II. Research Report. Report No. FHWA-RD-76-129. FHWA. Washington, DC, July 1979.

40. HANNA, JT, FLYNN, TE and TYLER, WK. Characteristics of intersection accidents in rural municipalities. Transportation Research Record 601. TRB. Washington, DC, 1976.

41. LOVEGROVE, SA. Approach speeds at uncontrolled intersections with restricted sight distances. J. Appl. Psychol. 63, pp. 635-42. Washington, DC, 1978.

42. LOVEGROVE, SA. Risk taking, approach speeds and traffic control at low volume intersections with restricted sight distances. Australian Road Research. Vol 9, No 2, Nunawading, Victoria, June 1979.

43. LERNER, N, WILLIAMS, A and SEDNEY, C. Risk perception in highway driving. Federal Highway Administration. Unpublished Report. FHWA. Washington, DC, May 1988.

44. KOSHI, M. Road safety measures in Japan. In Human behaviour and traffic safety pp. 27-41. Edited by Evans, L and Schwing, R. Plenum Press, New York, 1985.

Chapter IV

VEHICLE SAFETY

IV.1. INTRODUCTION

Behavioural adaptation occurs when a driver has become aware of the direct effects of design alterations to the vehicle on the safety system as a whole and permanently changes his driving behaviour accordingly. Evans (1) cites an explanation of this effect from Gibson and Crooks dating from 1938, which may be regarded as the earliest mention of behavioural adaptation:

> "... More efficient brakes on an automobile will not in themselves make driving the automobile any safer. Better brakes will reduce the absolute size of the minimum stopping zone, it is true, but the driver soon learns this new zone and, since it is his field-zone ratio which remains constant, he allows only the same relative margin between field and zone as before."

The same effect may be illustrated by a more recent example, the antilocking system (ALS) for brakes. It has been proposed that the antilocking system for brakes encourages a more reckless and forced style of driving, especially in critical situations. The prediction is justifiable in that behavioural adaptation may be observed in almost all areas of human life. However, if behavioural adaptation is to be used to explain the diminished effect of safety measures, it should be possible to state the reasons why the original aim was not achieved. That is, it should be possible to define the process which produced the behavioural adaptation.

Although significant safety benefits of technical innovations are frequently described and discussed in the relevant literature, only the design aims and technical effects of these innovations are discussed. As Danner (2) explains, it is nevertheless essential to make a clear distinction between:

-- The technical improvement and assessment of vehicle developments using technical measurements; and

-- The application of this technical progress in real traffic situations.

Estimates of the effects of innovations on driver behaviour, traffic flow or the incidence of accidents, let alone specific investigations of such effects, are rarely encountered in the scientific literature. The number of publications dealing with adaptations of driver behaviour is even smaller.

Even within this relatively small number of reports, a further distinction must be made according to whether behavioural adaptations are included as mere conjecture or by way of belated explanation, or whether they are specifically reflected in the hypothesis, design and implementation of the investigation.

The most extensively documented issue in the literature is behavioural studies on the seat belt and associated effects. Taken separately, the individual studies discuss only particular aspects of this issue and, for this reason, any evaluation of the adaptive processes is possible only if the individual results are collated and assessed together. Other examples from the field of vehicle safety (studded tyres, antilocking systems, etc.) are presented to provide examples of a range of behavioural adaptations.

At the end of the chapter an attempt is made to state criteria for the occurrence of behavioural adaptation processes as well as their magnitude and effect. These are derived from the results of the case studies and are intended to indicate to the practitioner when, or when not, to expect behavioural adaptation to occur.

IV.2. SAFETY FEATURES AND PERFORMANCE CHARACTERISTICS

During the last 25 years, numerous improvements to vehicle safety have been made as a result of the analysis of accident reports, ergonomic experience, and the results of research, particularly research on the kinetic and biomechanical effects of accidents on the human body. These results are reflected in passive (secondary) safety features, designed to minimise the effects of accidents, for example, deformation zones, reinforcement of the passenger compartment, improved windscreen fracture characteristics, improved restraint systems, and removal of sharp edges on controls.

Active (primary) safety features, on the other hand, designed to enhance handling performance and prevent accidents, have rarely been designed specifically for safety, but are often by-products in the improvement of vehicle performance. The constant increase in engine power led to increased speeds and called for corresponding safety measures, for example, in the drive, chassis or braking system of the vehicle.

Active safety features may be divided into four groups (3):

-- Conditional safety measures, which are designed to maintain the driver's physical and psychological capabilities;

-- Perception safety measures, which create the necessary conditions for seeing and being seen in road traffic;

-- Operating safety measures, which allow precise, rapid, and error-free control of the vehicle; and

-- Driving safety measures, which ensure that vehicle response is predictable and instantaneous and, if necessary, utilises the physical possibilites fully, including the control and stabilizing of the vehicle under normal and extreme conditions.

The first three areas have hitherto been considered mainly from the point of view of ergonomics. System-oriented investigations which go beyond driver-vehicle interaction are extremely rare, and behavioural adaptations in these areas are rarely mentioned. It would be conceivable, for example, for studies to be conducted into the relationship between improvements in driving comfort (improved suspension, better noise insulation, etc.) and driving behaviour. Improvements of this type are sometimes blamed for higher speeds, but practically no systematic investigations on this question are available. Nevertheless, the most important study results on current developments in conspicuity (daytime running lights, high-mounted braking lights) will be examined.

The fourth area, which includes in particular the control and stabilizing of the vehicle under different conditions, is often seen by vehicle researchers (technology) as a problem area in which it is often not possible to evaluate technical improvement without taking into account the reactions and adaptations of the driver. On the basis of extensive analysis of accidents classified according to vehicle type, Bock et al (4) conclude that the objective safety gain for a vehicle, which is often the aim, for example, of a more complicated chassis, is "usually" used by the driver to achieve greater speeds without subjectively incurring a greater risk. The greater engine power which usually accompanies such improvements creates the possibility of moving at ever-greater speeds.

The grading of premiums by accident insurance companies suggests that more powerful vehicles, which generally have better safety standards, have a higher level of damage claims than smaller vehicles. Of course, no causal relationship between engine power and involvement in accidents can be assumed without taking into account the relevant influencing variables. Many discrepancies can be accounted for by differences in driving intensity. Differences in driver personality also play a part in such statistics; drivers have particular motives for selecting a certain vehicle, preferring certain exposure conditions and particular styles of driving behaviour. Therefore, vehicle-oriented accident analyses always reflect the result of complex interactions of drivers, vehicles and circumstances.

In Germany, an investigation was recently completed into the connection between driver and vehicle characteristics and the incidence of accidents (5). The report contains a table of the accident rates, derived from police reports, of 70 different vehicle types. This was determined by the proportion of vehicles involved to the total of car accidents in one Land (Federal State of North Rhine-Westphalia, 1980), taking into account the average driving intensity (kilometres per annum) of each type of vehicle.

Vehicles with a high proportion of accidents include high-performance sporty vehicles, which also have good-quality active safety features. Major roads in particular have a surprisingly large number of accidents involving top-class vehicles which have not been spared any technical finesse in the field of active safety (best road holding, best brake systems). Vehicles with a lower proportion of the accidents include a considerable number of less powerful vehicles which, for the most part, are less well equipped with active safety features. While this section also includes vehicles with higher engine capacities, all of these are either lacking a particularly high-performance image or have adopted a particularly safety-conscious philosophy.

In the investigation referred to above (4), the authors used official vehicle and accident data (police records) from the state of North-Rhine-Westphalia (1980-82) to examine, as an example of active safety, the relationship between various types of wheel suspension systems and the incidence of accidents, modified to take into account different numbers of vehicles. They were unable to determine any positive effect provided by better wheel suspension systems. The vehicles with the most sophisticated chassis (twin control arms both front and rear) were, in relative terms, most involved in all accidents. The subdivision of accidents according to characteristics relating to driving performance also provided no evidence that the improved chassis technology was reflected positively in the accident statistics. Indeed, the results tended to show the opposite: better cars had worse accidents, especially on rural roads, where technical advantages should have the greatest effect. No causal relationships are proposed, and it is only possible to conclude that different wheel suspension systems are affected by other influencing variables.

Using two-dimensional evaluations of various vehicle parameters, the power-to-weight ratio of a vehicle (ratio of vehicle weight and engine power), which succinctly reflects the sporty design of a vehicle, proved to be particularly instructive. A decrease in the power-to-weight ratio was accompanied by a higher accident level. Furthermore, the number of accidents resulting from reasons of driving performance was also higher, despite the more sophisticated chassis technology which distinguishes sporty vehicles from normal ones.

Despite method-related restrictions associated with accident analyses of this type, it is evident that, in themselves, improvements in vehicle technology in the field of active safety revealed no corresponding effects with regard to road safety. Multivariate evaluations (LOGIT model) by the same authors demonstrated that vehicle-related characteristics could only help to explain an appreciable number of accidents in covariation with driver characteristics. These results moved the authors to propose the following:

"Measures to increase road safety must not be restricted solely to those designed at optimising vehicle technology, but must also integrate man's behaviour in this optimisation process. Measures restricted to the vehicle sector can even have a contrary result to that desired" (4).

Evans (1), in another study, comes to a similar conclusion. He establishes a clear difference between the physical safety of large and small vehicles and the safety actually found in accident analyses. From a technical viewpoint, the driver of a small vehicle (< 900 kg) is 2.6 times more likely to be killed in a single-car crash than the driver of a large vehicle (> 1 800 kg). However, accident analyses only revealed a probability ratio of 1.7. Evans concludes that this finding provides a clear reference to behavioural adaptations which reduce the technical disadvantages of small cars quite considerably.

According to Wasielewski and Evans (6), the indicators for behavioural adaptations may include less tailgating, lower speeds and increased seat belt use. These indicators express themselves in a generally more restrained, cautious style of driving. Extensive measurements on a no-speed-limit section of a German motorway (7) produced similar results. Apart from generally driving faster (higher speeds, greater use of overtaking lane), drivers of larger cars showed a distinct tendency to drive with dangerously short time intervals between vehicles. Evans and Herman (8) observed a test route to determine the time intervals which drivers accepted based on their vehicle's acceleration capabilities. Drivers accepted smaller intervals in cases where they had higher accelerating power. However, they did not sacrifice their safety advantage entirely. Brindle et al (9) observed overtaking procedures on major non-urban roads and established that drivers of "performance cars" were represented more than average in those cases when overtaking was least dangerous. The authors interpreted this result as evidence against behavioural adaptation. However, one could contend that increased driving intensity also gave rise to a large number of overtaking manoeuvres which, even on apparently safe sections of road, always imply more risks than simply driving in the normal traffic flow (10).

Summary

Evaluation studies have relied chiefly on the accident as the evaluation criterion for assessing behavioural adaptations. Measurements and observations have also been made in actual road traffic conditions to identify individual indicators of behavioural adaptations (headways, acceptance of time intervals between vehicles, overtaking). The safety benefit obtained through optimising devices for active vehicle safety could not be substantiated using universal accident figures. The technical improvements are affected by other influencing variables. The performance characteristics of the vehicle and personality variables of the driver are important factors which can lead to a riskier style of driving. This conclusion is also suggested by a number of individual behavioural studies.

IV.3. CONSPICUITY (DAYTIME RUNNING LIGHTS AND HIGH-MOUNTED BRAKING LIGHTS)

Daytime running lights and high-mounted braking lights are current measures designed to improve perception in road traffic. A feature common to both systems is that they do not extend the field of perception of the drivers themselves but instead provide other road users with improved information on driving events.

IV.3.1. Daytime running lights

Daytime running lights are intended to make vehicles more conspicuous during daytime driving and thereby decrease the detection time for daytime encounters in road traffic resulting in a reduction of the number of daytime collisions. The advantages are expected to be particularly significant for motorcycles, which are less conspicuous than passenger cars and are therefore "overlooked" more frequently.

Daytime running lights have been discussed primarily in the Scandinavian countries, Canada and the United States, and were partially introduced in the 1970s. The regulations covering their use differ from country to country. In some cases, they apply only to certain vehicle classes (such as motorcycles), to certain roads (rural), or times of the year (winter).

Numerous analyses have been conducted over recent years on the subject of daytime running lights. Despite different testing conditions, the results show a very high degree of concurrence (11, 12). Generally, positive effects are reported, but the increase in safety varies widely. Helmers estimates there is a reduction of approximately 11 per cent in the pertinent accidents (12).

Rumar (13) used experimental studies to demonstrate the advantages of daytime running lights, and he regards accident reductions reported in a Finnish and Swedish study as validation for his experimental studies. As early as 1975 it was shown that drivers perceive oncoming vehicles as closer than they really are when daytime running lights are being used. It addition, daytime running lights increased the range of peripheral vision (see 14).

A number of studies took into consideration the fact that the measure can also have undesirable side effects. For example, it has been shown that vehicles without daytime running lights are more difficult to perceive as surrounding lighting levels decline and as the number of vehicles with daytime running lights increases (12, 15, 16). In the accident analyses cited by Helmers (12), however, no corresponding disadvantage could be demonstrated on accident levels. Also, the hypothesis that the risk of accidents for pedestrians and two-wheelers, including motorcyclists, increases as the number of vehicles using daytime running lights increases was not confirmed. On the contrary, this group of road users seems to profit the most from the measure, as shown in various studies.

IV.3.2. High-mounted braking lights

High-mounted braking lights are designed to increase the ability of other drivers to detect braking of lead vehicles in order to reduce the incidence of rear-end collisions. The effectiveness of them has been demonstrated in a number of U.S. studies (17, 18, 19). Large scale field studies (18, 19) have shown decreases in accidents of between 44 per cent and 58 per cent using vehicles equipped with a centre, high-mounted braking light, which has shown to be the most effective design (20). All new passenger vehicles in North America now require this additional braking light. Initial results, based on police accident records, suggest a reduction of 22 per cent in the pertinent collision, compared with vehicles not equipped with the light (21). However, most studies have been unable to address the novelty effect these lights may have. Current thinking, not yet reported in relevant literature, is that some of the benefit from these lights is disappearing.

High-mounted braking lights were permitted in Germany since 1980. Unlike the North American version, the German system uses two lights even though this has been shown to be less effective (17, 22). The effectiveness of this system was studied using approximately 30 000 rear-end collisions recorded by the police in two federal states (23). Vehicles with high-mounted braking lights were involved in about 8 per cent of these collisions, but analyses failed to indicate any significant changes in accident occurrence due to the lights. However, it was found that the number of rear-end collisions in which both vehicles were equipped with high-mounted braking lights was around six times higher than expected (664 accidents vs. 108 expected accidents), and these accidents tended to be more serious. Marburger suggests behavioural adaptation as an explanation in "that drivers with brake lights, placing their confidence in the high-mounted braking lights of the lead vehicle, tend to drive with less headway, so that the mentioned rear-end collision constellation occurs more frequently" (23). Marburger based this interpretation on the results of a survey in which 54 per cent of drivers of vehicles fitted with high-mounted braking lights agreed with the statement that these lights were "so conspicuous" that it was "sufficient to drive with a smaller safety distance than usual" while only 25 per cent of drivers of nonequipped vehicles agreed with the statement (24). Possibly, the increased safety assumed by drivers resulted in a higher level of accident risk as a result of less careful driving -- a particularly critical form of behavioural adaptation.

Summary

The psycho-perceptual effects of daytime running lights and high-mounted braking lights were demonstrated by experimental studies (13 and 20, respectively). Effectiveness studies, based on accident data, produced very positive results, with the exception of the German study, which failed to determine any positive effect of high-mounted braking lights. In this study, the number of accidents in which both vehicles were fitted with high-mounted braking lights was significantly higher than the expected value. Behavioural adaptations explained in terms of risk compensation were put forward by the authors of the studies as a hypothesis for interpreting this result.

IV.4. STUDDED TYRES

Studded tyres have been developed for countries with ice- and snow-covered winter road conditions. Their primary advantages lie in their better track-holding properties and in considerably shorter braking distances, but these advantages apply only for ice- and snow-covered roads. Under other road conditions, as speed increases, lateral control is reduced and braking distances are extended by some 7 to 20 per cent (25). The greater safety expected of studded tyres can therefore only be attained if drivers do not drive more quickly on ice-covered roads than they do without studded tyres, and if they reduce their speeds and increase their following distances when the road is free of ice and snow.

Ernst and Hippchen (26) conducted a study in three regions of Germany using driving intensity and accident data for vehicles with and vehicles without studded tyres. During the study, the use of studded tyres ranged from 20 per cent to 42 per cent across the regions. Even though the roads were ice-covered only during part of the investigaion, the accident surveys revealed that vehicles with studded tyres were involved in 30 per cent less accidents than would have been expected from their share of road traffic. Similarly, Roosmark et al (27), on the basis of comparable accident data in Sweden, assessed the accident rate of vehicles with studded tyres during periods of snowfall at 60 per cent that of vehicles with normal tyres, and at 85 per cent in periods without snowfall. Overall, vehicles with studded tyres were involved in significantly fewer accidents than vehicles with regular tyres. However, there is a possibility that some of the accident reduction is due to driver characteristics. For example, safety conscious drivers who use studded tyres may be more likely to drive more slowly, even under good driving conditions.

Ernst and Hippchen also looked at accidents between vehicles with and without studded tyres, and assigned fault to one of the drivers. As was expected, drivers of vehicles with studded tyres were less likely to be at fault for the accident under conditions of ice and snow. When the road was free of snow and ice, however, more drivers of vehicles with studded tyres were at fault. Also, drivers of vehicles with studded tyres were more likely to collide with other vehicles on bare roads, and in accidents on icy roads these drivers, when at fault, were more likely to be taking greater risk (overtaking, passing, and encountering oncoming traffic) or being more negligent (turning manoeuvres and entering/leaving roads). These results suggest that drivers failed to adapt completely to the less favourable driving conditions on bare roads, and took too much advantage of the extra safety provided to them on ice and snow covered roads. Therefore vehicles with studded tyres would presumably show even greater safety benefits if it were not for behavioural adaptations.

In examining the reasons for the overall positive performance of vehicles with studded tyres, Krell refers to speed measurements conducted by Krebs et al (28). Measurements performed by the latter on ice free motorways revealed that vehicles with studded tyres in each vehicle class displayed lower 85 per cent speeds than drivers with normal tyres. The reductions in speed were sufficiently large to compensate for the increased braking distance. As the size of the vehicle increased, so did the safety margin over vehicles with normal tyres. From this, Krell concluded that "the low involvement of drivers of vehicles with studded tyres in accidents is attributable to the predominantly ice free roads", this being due in particular to reductions in the excessive speeds of vehicles with a large engine capacity.

There is some evidence that some of the differences in accidents between drivers with and drivers without studded tyres is due to driver characteristics such as age, driving experience and seat belt use (26). The size of the effect would suggest other explanations. Krell suggests that drivers with studded tyres drive more slowly because of sense of "loss of adhesion", and Pfafferott (29) established that these drivers are just as aware of the disadvantages of studded tyres on ice free roads as they are of the advantages of using these tyres when driving on ice. The increased noise from studded tyres on bare roads may also lead to greater caution, but the level of caution seems to extend beyond that dictated by the physical and technical conditions. This indicates a behavioural adaptation which enhances the safety effect of this measure, an advantage which the inventors of studded tyres had probably not envisaged.

To determine if drivers primarily fit studded tyres to increase safety or to increase speed on icy roads, the speeds of more than 6 000 vehicles with and without studded tyres were measured along two curves on a rural road under conditions of ice and no ice (30). On icy roads, it was discovered that drivers of vehicles with studded tyres tended to drive somewhat faster. However, the increase in speed did not reach the magnitude which would have been possible due to the increased tyre adhesion. As a result of behavioural adaptation, drivers apparently sacrificed part of their increased safety while retaining the supposedly greater part. The authors concluded that drivers primarily use studded tyres to increase their safety. In the same study, it was found that drivers who use studded types drive more slowly on normal tyres in the summer (30), suggesting that driver characteristics may also be responsible for lower accident rates amongst these drivers. The finding was not very pronounced and can scarcely be regarded as evidence for supporting the risk homeostasis theory as Kunkel (31) attempted to do.

Summary

Studies from Sweden and Germany have shown that vehicles with studded tyres are involved in fewer accidents than vehicles with normal tyres. The difference is particularly large when surfaces are covered with ice and snow, but also exists on dry or wet roads. Since roads are generally free of snow and ice even in winter, the safety benefit offered by studded tyres was -- paradoxically -- most effective for this type of road surface.

Speed measurements on icy and snow covered roads have established that drivers of vehicles with studded tyres drive slightly faster, and this was viewed as evidence of behavioural adaptation. Nevertheless, the improved grip offered by vehicles with studded tyres means that they still have a distinct safety advantage. Consequently, while the effect of the behavioural adaptation reduces the advantages of studded tyres on icy and snow-covered roads, these advantages are not cancelled out entirely.

Another major effect registered in Germany is that vehicles with studded tyres travelling on roads free of snow and ice achieve lower 85 per cent speeds than vehicles equipped with normal tyres. By adapting to the modified driving conditions, drivers of vehicles with studded tyres have evidently restricted their safety margin by driving at less-than-maximum speeds. The positive trend in accident figures in Germany has been attributed to a large extent to this behavioural adaptation.

Person-related influences have also been examined, but have been rated less important.

IV.5. ANTILOCKING SYSTEM (ALS)

Antilocking systems (ALS) make braking distances shorter and allow the vehicle to be steered even during the braking manoeuvres. These benefits are particularly effective in driving situations involving low or varying road adhesion, i.e., primarily on wet surfaces. Rompe, Schindler and Wallrich (32) examined the extent to which drivers exploit the increased steering and braking controllability allowed by ALS in simulated critical driving situations. ALS was shown to be beneficial in all investigated driving manoeuvres, with the advantages increasing as adhesion diminished. Over all, drivers without ALS made 2.4 times more errors (leaving a marked lane or striking an object on the road) than drivers with ALS.

Under the assumption that the simulated test conditions are equally relevant to accident incidence, the authors conclude that the early introduction of ALS on a universal basis would considerably reduce both the number and severity of road accidents. This in turn assumes that the average driver is given satisfactory instruction and training to make him adequately familiar with the new braking system. Behavioural adaptations were not investigated in this driving experiment, and no mention of such possibility was made. Langwieder (33) concluded, on the basis of accident studies, that the universal introduction of ALS in Germany could diminish the number of accidents involving severe damage to property and grave personal injury by 10 to 15 per cent.

Basing their investigations specifically on Wilde's risk homeostasis theory, Aschenbrenner, Biehl and Wurm (34) have tested the hypothesis that ALS does not help reduce accidents despite its technical benefits. This braking system, they claim, is one of a number of safety measures which do not directly influence risk acceptance. The authors set themselves the target of examining the effect of ALS under real traffic conditions. Their investigations were to incorporate attitudinal, behavioural and accident data to an equal degree.

A taxi company in Munich agreed to equip a number of its vehicles with ALS and provided a fleet of similar vehicles as a comparison group. The drivers were assigned randomly to the vehicles to avoid problems of self-selection (selective recruitment). The drivers were informed whether they were driving an ALS vehicle or not.

The results of this study do not provide a uniform picture:

-- The acceleration and deceleration data recorded with measuring apparatus showed no significant differences. During normal driving, vehicles both with and without ALS were accelerated and decelerated with almost the same intensity. The only difference was to be found at the extremes. ALS drivers decelerated very heavily slightly more often, whereas extreme acceleration values were more common with vehicles fitted with conventional braking systems. The authors interpret this rather as a direct technical consequence rather than as the result of behavioural changes.

-- Behavioural observations were conducted on a uniform stretch of road (113 journeys of 18 km). Observers were "camouflaged" as passengers and were unaware of whether the vehicle was fitted with ALS or not. The driving behaviour was assessed using 18 seven-step grading scales and differed significantly on four of the 18 variables under observation: drivers whose vehicles were fitted with ALS received less favourable assessments for the variables "cutting corners", "keeping to the lane", "anticipation" and "hazards". Furthermore ALS drivers drove distinctly faster than non-ALS drivers at one of four measuring points. In evaluating these differences, the authors concluded that drivers with ALS "tended" towards riskier driving.

-- With regard to the accident analyses, it is necessary to differentiate between an initial survey (1981 to 1983) which preceded the actual field experiment and covered 747 accidents involving vehicles with and without ALS (selected to exclude differences in driving intensities and seasonal variations), and a second survey (1985-86), which was performed as part of the field experiment and which included 51 accidents. Both analyses showed that drivers with ALS were involved in just as many accidents as drivers without ALS. However, the results showed that drivers with ALS were to blame for fewer accidents (at least in the initial accident survey). Further differences were:

.. ALS drivers were not involved in any accidents resulting from lateral collisions caused by other vehicles (whereas, in the case of taxis without ALS, 18 per cent of accidents for which the other vehicle was to blame took this form). This presumably reflects the greater manoeuvrability of ALS vehicles.

.. Under conditions of snow and ice, ALS drivers were to blame for more accidents than drivers without ALS. This is hardly surprising since the technical advantages of recent anti-locking systems were scarcely effective in ice and snow. However, the fact that ALS drivers had more accidents points to behavioural adaptations.

.. ALS drivers were apparently often able to avoid accidents due to the fact they were able to use the advantages of their braking system successfully in critical situations. There were considerably less ALS vehicles involved in accidents following full braking. This finding corroborates the expectations of Rompe et al, and Langwieder (32, 33).

.. On the other hand, ALS drivers were apparently less cautious in manoeuvres such as parking in restricted spaces and reverse parking, a situation reflected in a larger number of minor accidents.

.. With most other variables -- location, time of accident, other vehicles involved, speeds at the time of the accident, etc. -- no differences could be discerned between the two groups of vehicles.

The authors concluded that the results pointed to behavioural adaptations in the form of risk compensation since it was impossible to prove any universal increase in safety. While, for an equal number of accidents, the apportionment of blame was shifted from one group of drivers (ALS drivers) to other groups (initial accident survey), ALS drivers cancelled out the advantages offered by the ALS braking system by driving with less caution in other situations (second accident survey) (*).

Summary

In the ALS study (34), there were a number of indications of behavioural changes towards a riskier or less cautious manner of driving. The use of ALS did not change the number of accident involvements; however, ALS drivers were responsible for fewer accidents. There also seems to have been a shift towards minor accidents. Aschenbrenner et al conclude that only the combination of a large number of very different and subtle behavioural changes can explain the observed adaptations.

---

*   Statistics from insurance companies in Germany also show that vehicles equipped with ALS tend to have higher accident rates (accidents per person-kilometre) than vehicles of the same type which are not fitted with ALS. The self-selection of the drivers may well be the decisive factor in this respect (influence of driving style, person-related exposure conditions).

IV.6. SEAT BELTS

Studies worldwide demonstrate the effectiveness of seat belts and seat belt laws. Belts reduce vehicle occupant injuries which result from striking the steering wheel, the windscreen or other parts of the car and also reduce the risk of occupants being ejected from the vehicle. Studies suggest that wearing seat belts reduces the expected number of vehicle occupant fatalities by some 40 per cent to 50 per cent and considerably reduces the severity of injury (35, 36).

However, there are also a number of safety experts who remain sceptical as to the effect of seat belt laws or indeed even regard them in a negative light. For example, Conybeare (37) used accident trends in various states of Australia to demonstrate that, while the number of injuries and fatalities involving vehicle occupants was reduced as a result of seat belt laws and other safety measures incorporated in the vehicle, there was a significant rise in the number of injuries and fatalities for unprotected road users. He put forward the theory of an increase in the safety of vehicle occupants at the expense of non-occupants. To demonstrate this point, he cited a change in driver's risk perception which resulted in higher driving intensity and riskier driving. Adams (38) came to a similar conclusion as a result of performing time-series comparisons of fatality figures in countries with and without mandatory seat belt wearing laws. He was unable to determine any reduction in the number of fatalities in those countries which had enacted such laws. He, too, attributed this situation to behavioural adaptations on the part of the drivers. Protecting car occupants from the consequences of bad driving encourages bad driving, he concluded. This automatically increases the risk to pedestrians, cyclists and motorcyclists.

However, a number of counter-arguments have been put forward against these hypotheses. One such argument is that the theories postulated by Conybeare and Adams both attempted to provide explanations for historical phenomena and trends; in other words, their work represented ex-post explanations. Conybeare, for example, obtained the data for his studies over a long period (1949 to 1977), during which time Australia's safety system had been modified in so many ways that it would scarcely be possible to conclusively prove the effect or lack of effect of any individual variable.

The direct effect of the seat belts in reducing injury is of such a magnitude that behavioural adaptations, if such exist, ought to be readily apparent or should at least be detectable by scientific observation. In order to cancel out the direct benefit of the seat belt, belted drivers would have to:

-- Demonstrate a considerable reduction in risk perception or risk estimation; and/or

-- Adopt a distinctly more reckless manner of driving on the road.

However, this has not yet been demonstrated, and generally studies investigating behavioural adaptation tend to demonstrate the opposite. For example, Slovic, Fischhoff and Lichtenstein established in 1978 that the decision to wear a seat belt was attributable more to the probability of an accident occurring than to the magnitude of its consequences (39). Since the probability of an accident occurring does not, for the most part, depend on whether the driver wears a seat belt, belt usage ought not to have any (significant) effect on the driver's risk estimation. Any behavioural adaptation resulting from risk compensation may therefore be excluded (for the most part).

Bragg and Finn (40) determined that the assessment of danger in road traffic situations is no less for belted drivers than it is for non-belted drivers. With young drivers, fitting a seat belt before entering a traffic situation actually tended to increase their levels of risk estimation on the road.

Another study (41) used headway in high-flow motorway traffic as a measure of driver risk taking in conjunction with belt usage. Also, the authors compared belt use and headway in locations requiring belt use with that in locations not requiring belt use. Neither the belted user/non-belted user comparison nor the comparison of the various legal provisions provided any indication of significant differences in the choice of headway. Wearing a seat belt did not apparently result in riskier driving. Indeed, the data gathered tended to point to the contrary.

A study (42), conducted in the United Kingdom, using a large number of randomly selected passenger cars travelling on rural roads before seat belt usage became mandatory showed that the average speed of belted drivers was 1 mph higher than that of non-belted drivers. Other factors, however, such as vehicle size, vehicle age or the presence of passengers, influenced speeds more significantly. If one considers that drivers of larger and newer vehicles wore seat belts more frequently, but that higher mean speeds were measured for these vehicles, one can conclude that, assuming the "vehicle size" and "vehicle age" remained constant, belted drivers were more likely to achieve lower mean speeds than non-belted drivers.

No studies could be traced which deal with additional indicators of driving behaviour relating to belt usage and which, to a large extent, exclude the special personality differences of belt users/non-belt users. We have therefore based our discussions below on accident analyses explicitly incorporating considerations according to behavioural adaptations.

The question of risk shifting to other road user groups played a central role in the political discussion around the introduction of mandatory seat belt wearing in the United Kingdom. Particular emphasis was therefore placed on this criterion within the framework of the accompanying analyses into the effectiveness of seat belts (43). In the belief that any increase in driver risk taking resulting from belt usage amongst passenger car drivers ought to be reflected in the number of accidents involving unprotected road users, accident data before the introduction of the mandatory seat belt laws were used to predict accident figures for the period following the enactment of the seat belt law.

The study differentiated between how often unprotected road users collided with a) passenger cars which were subject to the mandatory seat belt law and b) public service vehicles (PSV) and heavy freight vehicles (HFV) which were excluded from the law. The pattern of accidents provided no evidence to support the theory of risk shifting. The number of accidents between unprotected road users and passenger car drivers in the post-belt period corresponded to the predicted figures, as did the number of accidents involving unprotected road users and PSV/HFV. Deviations from the predicted values were shown to lie within the range of random scatter. Scott and Wallis were able to conclude that there had apparently been no behavioural adaptation resulting from the seat belt laws or an associated shifting of risk at the expense of other road users.

Similar results have been reported from Switzerland and Germany. The first time that compulsory seat belt wearing was introduced in Switzerland (it was invalidated after approximately one and a half years for legal reasons), as well as the second time, the number of injured and killed car passengers diminished significantly. During this period, the number of injured and killed pedestrians also decreased and, in the case of the bicycle and motor-cyclists, the trend continued as before (44). Based on recent statistics, there has been no change in these findings since the use of seat belts became compulsory for the second time.

Accident trends in Germany (number of fatalities in the year before and after the mandatory seat belt law was enacted) also do not support the theory of risk shifting. The number of passenger car driver fatalities fell by 32 per cent in the "after" period (1985) compared with the "before" period (1983). The number of unprotected road user deaths also showed no increase and, indeed, fell by 27 per cent. While this does not disprove the risk shifting theory, it is nevertheless extremely improbable that detailed accident studies would be able to find any evidence to support it in view of the almost parallel drops in the number of fatalities for passenger car drivers and unprotected road users. The fall in the fatality figures for unprotected road users was continued in subsequent years. Janssen (45) attempted to prove that the actual safety gain in Germany through using the seat belt has turned out to be considerably less than expected, but his conclusions have been called into question (46).

Ernst (46) concedes that it is possible that the safety gain is slightly less than originally expected, but it would appear speculative to attribute this to behavioural adaptations without seriously examining other, more obvious possible explanations. It is thus conceivable that the expected values derived from medical-technical studies into belt efficiency were set too high.

Differences in daytime and nighttime seat belt use and selective recruitment, as demonstrated by Evans (47), might also account for the failure to achieve desired safety benefits. There is also some evidence that belt use tends to heighten the caution shown by the driver. Buckling a seat belt may be a timely reminder of the ever-present risk of accidents (1, 48). An experimental investigation by Streff and Geller (49) showed that a group of drivers who had been unbelted in a first experimental phase increased their speed once the belts were fitted and that another group of drivers, who were belted in the first phase, slowed down when no longer wearing belts.

Summary

It was predicted that wearing a seat belt increases the driver's subjective sense of security and causes him to take more risks when driving. The variables applied to determine behavioural adaptations encompassed:

-- Accident figures (reduction in occupant casualties at the expense of other road users);
-- Driving behaviour (speed, headway);
-- Attitudes (perception and estimation of risks).

The projected behavioural adaptations were based on theoretical considerations (risk homeostasis) on the one hand and on the results of universal accident comparisons on the other hand.

The hypotheses were not confirmed conclusively in any study examining behavioural adaptations. It cannot therefore be assumed that the safety benefits associated with wearing seat belts are reduced as a result of behavioural adaptations, but expected gains in safety are also not completely realised). No evidence could be found at either the risk estimation or behavioural observation level that drivers took more risks when wearing seat belts. It might have also been possible to investigate more subtle criteria of behavioural adaptation (e.g. more cautious driving or a lower degree of attention) -- but this has not been done.

IV.7. DISCUSSION

The purpose of this chapter was to summarise the study results on behavioural adaptations for safety-related vehicle features. The safety aspects and measures which were examined in detail encompassed the performance characteristics/road safety of the vehicle, daytime running lights, high-mounted braking lights, studded tyres, the antilocking system (ALS,) and safety belts. The examples selected were determined primarily by the literature available on the given subject.

In a number of cases, studies on the effect of vehicle safety features produced convincing results. This is particularly true for the seat belt, but also applies for improvements in the field of perception safety. In the studies conducted on studded tyres and ALS, evidence of increased safety was often accompanied by behavioural adaptations which affect the efficiency of the individual measures -- in some cases enhancing them, in others reducing them. There is evidence to indicate that safety measures, such as improved vehicle technology, that are passed on to the driver along with improved vehicle performance (speed, acceleration values) do not result in any increase in road safety. In such instances, the behavioural adaptation aspect is already an integral component of the design concept. Table IV.1. summarises the results of the literature analysis.

Accident analyses alone generally do not contribute to an understanding of behavioural adaptation. It has been shown that other explanations may be more reasonable than those suggesting behavioural adaptation. However, this may be a problem more associated with the analysis of safety effects using aggregate data rather than behavioural data.

Table IV.1

SAFETY EFFECT, INFLUENCE AND DIRECTION OF BEHAVIOURAL ADAPTATION

Safety measure	Safety Effect	Influence of Behavioural Adaptation	Direction of Behavioural Effect
Primary safety in conjunction with sporty vehicle design	Negative if any	Proven	Negative
Daytime running lights	Positive	Not proven	--
High-mounted braking lights	Positive	Suggested	If present, negative
Studded tyres	Positive	Proven	Positive & negative
Antilocking system	Not proven	Proven	Negative
Seat belts	Positive	Not proven (often suspected from accident comparisons)	--

In order to overcome the more hypothetical character of accident data, every effort should be made to create a link between the measure (input) and the accident (output). Behavioural observations and questionnaire data make it possible to describe the process of behavioural adaptation. As, for example, the behavioural observations for driving with a seat belt have shown, the hypothesis of behavioural adaptation derived from aggregate data receives little support from observational data. Speed measurements on the other hand have provided a valuable contribution to understanding accident trends and revealing behavioural adaptations resulting from the use of studded tyres.

As the various behavioural analyses of the German ALS study showed, not all behavioural adaptation processes can be expected to be easily identifiable and recordable. It is quite conceivable that adaptations can only be determined from a large number of very different and subtle behavioural modifications. In this context (10, 34), authors quote motivational, information-processing, attitude-related and knowledge-based changes in the driver which can interact in complex ways. This fact should be borne in mind for future studies on vehicle-related behavioural adaptations.

The question we are now facing is whether the individual studies available can be used to derive general information on the conditions which can be expected to result in behavioural adaptations and whether the adaptation in question tends to reduce or increase the intended effect. A tentative attempt will be made to answer this question at the end of this section.

Interaction with the Measures

The behavioural adaptation process to new vehicle conditions require the driver to interact with these conditions. A minimum requirement for behavioural adaptations is that the driver perceives - more or less consciously - the effect of a measure (or at least is informed of this effect) and that he himself can react to it. We can exclude the possibility of there being adaptations to vehicle features, the effect of which the driver is unable to sense or even know of. For example, a windscreen with improved accident protection characteristics will not likely to result in behavioural adaptation if drivers are unaware of it.

Immediacy of the Feedback

One central hypothesis for explaining the different behavioural adaptation processes in drivers of vehicles with studded tyres was the immediacy of the feedback they receive from it, such as changed travel dynamics and increased noise level. The lack of feedback ("lack of sensory certainty") on the positive effect of the seat belt was quoted among other points as a reason for the low willingness to wear belts (48). However, it is probably this missing feedback which is partially responsible for the fact that the behavioural adaptations envisaged by Conybeare (37) and Adams (38) resulting from high belt-wearing quotas did not materialise. Behavioural adaptations to a safety measure is more pronounced when, amongst other things, the driver has clear feedback on the effects of the measure or, at the very least, has information about these effects (i.e. knowledge of what should happen).

Extending the Freedom of Action

At the start of research work into related literature, it was assumed that the probability for effect-reducing behavioural adaptations could be assessed according to whether primary or secondary vehicle safety characteristics were involved. However, this differentiation is inadequate, as evidenced by the various findings on perception and driving safety. It would be more appropriate to employ a method of differentiation which uses the driver's freedom of action as its criterion. The improved chassis technology accompanying an increase in the power of a vehicle has the purpose of extending the driver's freedom of action (new fields of action, higher speeds, more extreme curves, etc.). However, daytime running lights which improve the noticeability of a car do not affect the freedom of action of the driver himself. There is therefore less probability of direct behavioural adaptation on the part of the driver.

Increase in Subjective Safety

As the example of studded tyres showed, feedback on the disadvantages of a safety measure tend to result in behavioural adaptations which increase safety levels because subjective safety is lowered. In contrast to this, behavioural adaptations resulting in reduced safety levels may well result when subjective safety is increased. In cases of this type, the driver believes that he is better equipped and is therefore better able to handle critical situations. This has been demonstrated with studded tyres on ice and snow, with the ALS, and with German studies into high-mounted braking lights.

Superimposing of the Driving Goals by Extra Motives

In the final analysis, behavioural adaptations are governed by the driving goals pursued by a driver. Drivers employ the vehicle technology available to them in order to suit their driving purpose, motivation, driving style and current psychic process. The greater the availability of technical features in the terms of "joy of driving" (48) or "extra motives" (50), the more likely it is that these features will be used for reasons other than technical safety. This has been demonstrated first and foremost by studies into the relationship between vehicle size, vehicle safety and the incidence of accidents. On the other hand, it can be assumed that the danger of behavioural adaptations resulting in reduced safety levels is least pronounced when the driver has a well developed awareness of safety.

In conclusion, the points raised to date will be summarised for the benefit of persons operating at a practical level, e.g. vehicle designers. If they wish to know whether a planned design measure on the vehicle will result in undesirable adaptational processes, they should ask themselves the following questions:

1. Will the driver perceive the change?
   If not, no adaptational processes are to be expected (or they will take considerable time to develop).

2. Will the driver become directly aware of the change during driving?
   If yes, adaptational processes can be expected. If the driver does not receive any immediate feedback, but is informed of the ffect, behavioural adaptations cannot be excluded. However, these are only likely if a number of the following criteria apply.

3. Is the change able to extend the driver's freedom of action?
   For example, will he look for new driving settings (all-wheel drive, studded tyres, etc.)? Can he drive more quickly, overtake more easily, etc.?
   If yes, adaptational processes can be expected.

4. Does the change increase the subjective safety of the driver, i.e. does the driver feel more in charge of driving situations?
   If yes, adaptational processes can be expected.

5. Does the change fit in with driving aims relating to driving pleasure, a liking for high speeds, "thrills", a will to dominate, etc.?
   If yes, adaptational processes can be expected.

This list of questions is naturally only a basic framework. It is only intended to provide a general outline as to whether adaptational processes can be expected or not. The direction of the adaptational process (more or less safety) can be roughly deduced from examining the individual criteria as a whole. However, linear relationships between design changes on the vehicle and behavioural adaptations may not be assumed, due to the narrow empirical base involved.

The degree to which this list of criteria can be further developed and defined in greater detail depends not least on a broad spectrum of research being conducted into the effects of safety measures and behavioural adaptations in this field. Brown (51) referred to the need for greater research in the interface between man and technology when, under ergonomic criteria, he listed conditions of "danger compensation" which come very close to those referred to here.

REFERENCES

1.   EVANS, L. Human behaviour feedback and traffic safety. Human Factors, 27. 555-576. Santa Monica, 1985.

2.   DANNER, M. Der Mensch im Gesamtsystem Fahrzeug/Umwelt. Zeitschrift für Verkehrssicherheit, 27 (2). Darmstadt, 1981.

3.   DONGES, E. Beitrag der Kraftfahrzeugtechnik zur Aktiven Sicherheit des Strassenverkehrssystems. Verkehrsunfall und Fahrzeugtechnik, 23 (9), 251-256. Kippenheim, 1985.

4.   BOCK, O, BRUEHNING, E, DILLING, J, ERNST, G, MIESE, A and SCHMID, M. Aufbereitung und Auswertung von Fahrzeug-und Unfalldaten Schriftenreihe Unfall und Sicherheitsforshung strassenverkehr, Heft 74, Bergisch Gladbach, 1989.

5.   DOERSCHLAG, S, SCHLICHTING, KD. Fahrer- und Fahrzeugeigenschaften und Unfallgeschehen. Forschungsbericht für die Bundesanstalt für Strassenwesen, FP 8015. Braunschweig, 1987.

6.   WASIELEWSKI, P and EVANS, L. Do drivers of small cars take less risk in everyday driving? Risk Analysis, 5 (1). 25-32 New York, 1985.

7.   BRUEHNING, E. Zum Verkehrsverhalten in Abhängigkeit vom gefahrenen Fahrzeugtyp. Strassenverkehrstechnik 17, 85-90. Bonn-Bad Godesberg, 1973.

8.   EVANS, L and HERMAN, R. Note on driver adaptation to modified vehicle starting acceleration. Human Factors, 18, 235-240. Santa Monica, 1976.

9.   BRINDLE, LR, HARRIS, D and MUIR, H. Driver overtaking behaviour -- an observational study. Contemporary Ergonomics, 98-102. London, 1986.

10. ASCHENBRENNER, M, BIEHL, B and WURM, G. Einfluss der Risikokompensation auf die Wirkung von Verkehrssicherheitsmassnahmen am Beispiel ABS. In: Schriftenreihe Unfall- und Sicherheitsforschung Strassenverkehr, Heft, 63. 65-70. Bergisch Gladbach, 1988.

11. HENDERSON, RL, ZIEDMAN, K, BURGER, WJ and CAVEY, KE. Motor vehicle conspicuity. SAE Technical Paper Series 830566. Detroit, 1983.

12. HELMERS, G. Daytime running lights -- a potent traffic safety measure? Report 333A. Swedish Road and Traffic Research Institute (VTI). Linköping, 1988.

13. RUMAR, K. Running lights -- conspicuity, glare and accident reduction. Accident Analysis and Prevention, 12, 151-157. Oxford, 1980.

14. KURATORIUM FÜR VERKEHRSSICHERHEIT (KfV). Licht bei Tag. Vienna, 1988.

15. ATTWOOD, DA. Daytime running lights project. V: Effect of headlight glare on the detection of unlit vehicles. RSU Technical Report No. 77/1. Defense and Civil Institute of Environmental Medicine. Toronto, 1977.

16. ATTWOOD, DA. The effects of headlight glare on vehicle detection at dusk and dawn. Human Factors, 21 (1). Santa Monica, 1979.

17. KOHL, JS and BAKER, C. Field test evaluation of rear lighting systems, DOT contract No. HS-05-01228. Washington, DC, February 1978.

18. REILLY, RE, KURKE, WS and BUCKENMAIER, CC. Validation of the reduction of rear-end collisions by a high-mounted auxiliary stoplamp. DOT contract No. HS-7-01756. Washington, DC, May 1980.

19. RAUSCH, A and KIRKPATRICK, M. A field test of two single centre, high-mounted brake light systems. Accident Analysis and Prevention. 14, (4), 287-291, Oxford, 1982.

20. SIVAK, M, CONN, LS and OLSON, PL. Driver eye fixations and the optimal locations for automobile brake lights. Journal of Safety Research, 17(1), 13-22. Chicago, 1986.

21. KAHANE, CJ. The effectiveness of centre high-mounted stop lamps. A preliminary evaluation. National Highway Traffic Safety Administration. Technical Report, HS 807076. Washington, DC, 1987.

22. FAERBER, B. Wahrnehmungspsychologische Fragen zu den hochgesetzten Bremsleuchten. Psychologisches Institut der Universität Tübingen. Tübingen, 1982.

23. MARBURGER, EA. Zum Einfluss zusätzlicher hochgesetzter Bremsleuchten auf das Unfallgeschehen. Forschungsberichte der Bundesanstalt für Strassenwesen, Bereich Unfallforschung. Heft 108, Bergisch Gladbach, 1984.

24. WEISSBRODT, G. Repräsentativerhebung zur Bewertung der hochgesetzten Bremsleuchten durch Pkw-Fahrer. Bundesanstalt für Strassenwesen. Köln, 1982.

25. KRELL, K. Der Einfluss von Spike-Reifen auf die Verkehrssicherheit und die Umwelt. Strasse und Autobahn, Heft 10, 1-7. Bonn-Bad Godesberg, 1973.

26. ERNST, R and HIPPCHEN, L. Untersuchungen über den direkten Einfluss von Spikes-Reifen auf das Unfallgeschehen, Teil b: Unfallbeteiligung spikesbereifter Fahrzeuge. Schriftenreihe Strassenbau und Strassenverkehrstechnik. Heft 170, 115-147. Bonn-Bad Godesberg, 1974.

27. ROOSMARK, PO, ANDERSSON, K and AHLQVIST, G. The effect of studded tyres on traffic accidents. Report No. 72. National Swedish Road and Traffic Research Institute. Linköping, 1976.

28. KREBS, HG, LAMM, R and LEUTNER, R. Das Geschwindigkeitsverhalten von Pkw mit und ohne Spike-Bereifung. In: Schriftenreihe Strassenbau und Strassenverkehrstechnik, Heft 170. Bonn-Bad Godesberg, 1974.

29. PFAFFEROTT, I. Psychische Einflussgrössen für die Einhaltung oder Übertretung einer Geschwindigkeitsbeschränkung. Diss. an der Universit t Köln. Köln, 1974.

30. RUMAR, K, BERGGRUND, U, JERNBERG, P and YTTERBOM, U. Driver reaction to a technical safety measure -- studded tyres. Human Factors, 18, 443-454. Santa Monica, 1976.

31. KUNKEL, E. Theorie der Risikohomoeostase. In: Gfs-Sicherheitswissenschaftliche Monographie, Bd. 6. Wuppertal, 1984.

32. ROMPE, K, SCHINDLER, A and WALLRICH, M. Advantages of an anti wheel lock system (ABS) for the average driver in difficult driving situations. XIth International Technical Conference on Experimental Safety Vehicle. Washington, DC, 1987.

33. LANGWIEDER, K. Der Problemkreis Bremsen in der Unfallforschung. VII. -Symposium. HUK -Verband, Büro Für Kfz-Technik, München, 1986.

34. ASCHENBRENNER, M, BIEHL, B and WURM, G. Mehr Verkehrssicherheit durch bessere Technik? Felduntersuchungen zur Risikokompensation am Beispiel des Antiblockiersystems (ABS). Mannheim, 1988.

35. HEDLUND, J. Casualty reductions resulting from safety belt use laws. In: Effectiveness of safety belt use laws: A multinational examination, NHTSA, 73-97. Washington, DC, 1985.

36. MARBURGER, EA and MEYER, L. Wirksamkeit des Sicherheitsgurtes und Entwicklung der Anlegequoten in der Bundesrepublik Deutschland. Zeitschrift für Verkehrssicherheit, 32 (2), 82-91. Darmstadt, 1986.

37. CONYBEARE, JAC. Evaluation of automobile safety regulations: the case of compulsory seat belt legislation in Australia. Policy Sciences 12, 27-39. Amsterdam, 1980.

38. ADAMS, JGU. The efficacy of seat belt legislation. Society of Automotive Engineers, SAE Paper No. 820819. Warrendale, PA, 1982.

39.   SLOVIC, P, FISCHHOFF, B and LICHTENSTEIN, S.   Accident probabilities
        and seat belt usage: a psychological perspective.   Accident Analysis
        and Prevention, 10, 281-285. Oxford, 1978.

40.   BRAGG, BWE and FINN, P.   Influence of safety belt usage on perception
        of the risk of an accident. Accident Analysis and Prevention, 17 (1),
        15-23. Oxford, 1985.

41.   EVANS, L, WASIELEWSKI, P v. BUSECK, CR.   Compulsory seat belt usage and
        driver risk-taking behaviour.   Human Factors, 24 (1), 41-48. Santa
        Monica, 1982.

42.   MACKAY, GM, DALE, KJ and WHITE, A.   Seat belts under a voluntary
        regime: Some aspects of use related to occupant and vehicle
        characteristics and driving behaviours.   Proceedings of the VIIth
        IRCOBI Conference on Biomechanics of Impacts. Lyon, 1982.

43.   SCOTT, PP, and WALLIS, PA.   Road casualties in Great Britain during the
        first year with seat belt legislation. Research Report No. 9. TRRL.
        Crowthorne, 1985.

44.   AKTIONSKOMITEE F R DAS TRAGEN DER SICHERHEITSGURTEN, SCHWEIZ.
        Referentenführer zur eidg. Volksabstimmung. Schweiz, Beratungsstelle
        für Unfallverhütung bfu. Bern, 1980.

45.   JANSSEN, WH. Gurtanlegequoten und Kfz-Insassen-Sicherheit. Zeitschrift
        für Verkehrssicherheit 34, (2), 65-67. Darmstadt, 1988.

46.   ERNST, R.   Gurtanlegequoten und Kfz-Insassen-Sicherheit.   Zeitschrift
        für Verkehrssicherheit 34, (4), 185-186. 3. Darmstadt, 1988.

47.   EVANS, L.   Estimating fatality reductions from increased safety belt
        use. Risk Analysis, 7, 49-57. New York, 1987.

48.   BERGER, HJ, BLIERSBACH, G, DELLEN, RG, KROJ, G and PFAFFEROTT, I.
        Psychologische Forschung zum Sicherheitsgurt und Umsetzung ihrer
        Ergebnisse.   Schriftenreihe   Unfall-   und   Sicherheitsforschung
        Strassenverkehr. Heft 2. Köln, 1974.

49.   Streff, FM and Geller, ES.   An experimental test of risk compensation:
        between-subject versus within-subject analysis. Accident Analysis and
        Prevention, 20, (4), 277-287, Oxford, 1988.

50.   NAATANEN, R and SUMMALA, H.   Road user behaviour and traffic accidents.
        North-Holland Publishing Cy. Amsterdam, 1976.

51.   BROWN, ID.   Can ergonomics improve primary safety in road transport
        systems? Ergonomics, 22, No. 2. London, 1979.

Chapter V

<u>EDUCATION AND ENFORCEMENT</u>

V.1.   INTRODUCTION

The purpose of this Chapter is to discuss behavioural adaptation in the context of traffic safety measures aimed at improving traffic by directly changing the behaviour of the road user. For convenience the traffic safety measures will be divided into three groups. The first group consists of publicity campaigns. These campaigns, which operate by means of mass media, are aimed at increasing traffic safety by informing road users about certain conditions or by persuading them to change a certain behaviour or attitude. The second group consists of education and training. These formal programmes are aimed at increasing traffic safety by means of (theoretical) education and/or practical training. The third group consists of attempts to change the behaviour of the road users by means of legislation and enforcement, for instance, seat belt laws, helmet laws, etc.

It should be stressed that the research results presented in this Chapter are a selection of studies and not a complete review. Two selection criteria were used. The first and most important criterion was that the studies presented should be methodologically sound. The second criterion was that the studies should be interesting in the context of this report, that is, they should provide information of use for evaluating the existence and the extent of behavioural adaptation. The second criterion led to an overrepresentation of studies showing negative safety effects. However, this apparent bias has been taken into consideration in the development of the conclusions presented for the Chapter.

There are a number of problems associated with a review of the effects of these safety measures. First, the classification of safety measures made in this Chapter is much wider and more heterogeneous than in the preceding chapters on vehicles and highway safety. This is evident if one compares the safety measure "studded tyres" with the safety measure "publicity campaigns." The effects of studded tyres on friction can be described in a homogeneous way, both in theory and in practice. It is therefore reasonable to consider studded tyres as one safety measure. That is, in a taxonomy for road safety measures, "studded tyres" is a natural class.

However, if you look at publicity campaigns as a safety measure, the picture is somewhat different. The only thing that really is common for different publicity campaigns is the use of mass media for distributing "something." The content of the campaigns, the target populations, etc., are quite different from one campaign to another, making it difficult to derive general conclusions. The situation is exactly the same for the other two areas in this Chapter: education and training, and legislation and enforcement. Under each heading you will find separate safety measures that will differ to a considerable extent on both intuitive and more objective criteria. The obvious solution to this problem would be to use a better taxonomy for the safety measures in this Chapter. However, a better taxonomy is not available.

Another problem associated with the safety measures discussed in this Chapter is the difficulty of identifying, describing and separating the intended effects of the measures from the unintended effects. As was seen in Chapter II, this is a very important step in the identification of behavioural adaptation. There are at least two elements of this problem. Firstly, it is difficult in this context to know if a safety measure actually has an initial effect. If the design of the braking system of a car is changed, or an intersection is rebuilt, it is very clear that something has actually been done, but if something is changed in the training of new drivers or in posters telling drivers to be more careful are put up, it is not clear that the target population has been reached. Therefore, a lack of safety effect may not, necessarily, be an indication of behavioural adaptation. The intended positive effects may not have been counteracted by an unintended negative effect, but rather it could be that the lack of effect was due to problems with the implementation of the safety measure. Secondly, with these types of safety measures it is seldom explicitly stated what the mechanisms are that will cause safety improvements. In the "studded tyre" example, the mechanism that is intended to make driving safer is the following: studded tyres give better friction, which leads to better manoeuvrability of vehicles, which leads to safer driving. For the safety measures in this Chapter, the mechanisms are seldom this clear.

For example, a Swedish publicity campaign, aimed at increasing the traffic safety of children, stated that the goal should be reached by a) "increasing the knowledge of adults regarding children's limited ability to cope with traffic," and b) "making all road users respect and take responsibility for children's safety in traffic" (1). This is not a clear statement of the mechanisms by which this campaign should affect safety, but at least it implies the following mechanism: if adult road users to a larger extent believe that children are incapable road users, and this belief is, in some way, transformed into action, then the safety of the children will increase. Now, consider the following hypothetical outcome of the campaign: an evaluation shows i) intended effects on a) increased awareness of children's limited ability to deal with traffic and on b) all road users aware of their responsibility for child safety, but ii) no effect on children's safety in traffic. This result could be explained by either behavioural adaptation or by an application of ineffective mechanisms. Behavioural adaptation would be the explanation if the positive safety effects caused by a) and b) were counteracted by a third mechanism, not originally taken into consideration. Ineffective mechanisms would be the explanation if the basic reasoning behind the effects of a) and b) was faulty, i.e., that a) and b) do not lead to increased safety.

In summary, there could be at least three different reasons for a lack of effect of these safety measures:

        -- Ineffective implementation of safety measure;
        -- Reliance on ineffective mechanisms;
        -- Behavioural adaptation.

        This Chapter will focus on the identification of behavioural adaptation
as a reason behind unwanted or unexpected effects of road user programmes.
When the lack of effect cannot be attributed to behavioural adaptation because
no behavioural data were collected, the results of the studies will be
reviewed to determine if ineffective implementation or ineffective accident
reducing mechanisms were the causes of the failure.

V.2.   PUBLICITY CAMPAIGNS

        The following section summarises some of the effects of publicity
campaigns and also suggests why these campaigns do not always have the
predicted effect. The mediating mechanisms vary from campaign to campaign,
but the most common one is that an attitude change will produce a change in
behaviour. Campaigns can also be used to change the behaviour of road users
in a more direct manner by suggesting a new behaviour and presenting the
benefits associated with it. Other uses can also be made of publicity
campaigns; for example, they can be used for introducing new legislation, a
function that will be discussed in Section V.4.

        One of the attractive features of publicity campaigns is the relatively
low cost compared with the potential gains. For instance, Lalani & Holden
report a reduction in accident costs, from a campaign on motorcyclist
conspicuity, of approximately 200 times the cost for the campaign (2). The
large effect is in part due to the use of mass media, which means that, if the
campaign has an effect, the effect is delivered to a large proportion of the
population. As another example, the cost of an average Swedish publicity
campaign equals the cost of one to three deaths due to traffic accidents.
Publicity campaigns are therefore often seen as attractive safety measures.

        However, publicity campaigns are seldom proved to be effective, partly
because of the difficulties in evaluating them. Evaluations frequently are
before-after designs without proper control conditions. Without good
evaluation studies, it is difficult to prove the benefits from any safety
measure.

        Even when proper designs are used positive effects can be difficult to
demonstrate. Andersson (3) reports on a good evaluation of seven traffic
safety booklets. Five of the booklets were characterized as traditional,
educational type material, describing hazards to safe driving (e.g., alcohol,
speeding) and how to minimize these hazards. One of these five booklets was
designed to be of value for all drivers regardless of their age or sex, and
the remaining four were specially designed for specific age and sex groups. A
sixth booklet contained material stressing the human factor in driving, such
as emotions, attitudes and physical states, and tried to increase reader
awareness of the importance of these factors in safe driving. The seventh
booklet concentrated on highway signs and street markings, describing their
meaning and where they are normally seen.

The seven booklets were distributed to seven experimental groups by mail. A letter was enclosed, stressing the need to reduce accidents, explaining that the purpose of the booklet was to make the reader a better driver, and encouraging the reader to read the booklet several times. The design also included two control groups; one dummy contact control group, and a pure control group. The dummy contact control group received a letter asking the receivers to send in their new address if there had been a recent change in address. In total, 92 000 subjects were used in the design.

The effects of the traffic safety booklets on driver behaviour were evaluated, using both accidents and traffic convictions. No significant effects were found. It was concluded that these types of safety materials should not be used in traffic safety programmes. The main reason behind the failure was, according to the author, motivational. The subjects were not motivated to read the material, nor were they motivated to make the changes suggested in the material.

In 1976 the Swedish Traffic Safety Administration launched a campaign called "Children in Traffic" (1), focussing on children's limited abilities to cope with traffic. The main message was that, due to the limited abilities of children, the adults have the full responsibility for their safety. The campaign materials consisted of about 50 different posters, pamphlets, stickers, etc. The evaluation of the campaign showed that the main message was received by the general public as measured by an attitude questionnaire distributed before and after the campaign. However, no conclusions about the effects of the campaign on accidents were presented in the report. Elofsson analysed accident data and concluded that it was unlikely that the campaign had any short term effects on accidents (4).

In Norway a nationwide campaign was launched in 1985, called "Better Driving 85" (5). The aim of the campaign was to change the driving behaviour of ordinary drivers and to reduce the number of accidents. The objective was to be achieved by increased surveillance on the road by the police and by vehicle inspectors, and by informing drivers about accident risks and the causes of traffic accidents. The campaign was evaluated by looking first at the activity of the vehicle inspectors and the police. Secondly, the drivers' perceived risk of apprehension was measured. Thirdly, the headways of vehicles were measured before and during the campaign. The investigation also tried to find out if the accident rates had changed due to the campaigns. The results showed that the vehicle inspectors had increased their activities during the campaign, but this was not the case for the traffic police. However, no effects due to the campaign could be found on drivers' perceived risk of apprehension, the headways of vehicles, or the accident rates. The author therefore concludes that the campaign did not attain its goals.

Downing and Spendlove report an evaluation of the effects of a campaign to reduce accidents involving children crossing roads near parked cars, called "Operation Dash Out" (6). The campaign consisted of two parts, one directed towards the children and one directed towards the drivers. Every primary and middle school in the campaign area received a pack of road safety teaching material including local accident information, a poster showing the campaign logo, explanatory notes about the campaign and its aims, and a variety of teaching suggestions including directions for how to practise safe road crossing. The evaluation of the campaign showed no change in children's crossing behaviour on their journeys to and from school. There was, however, improvement on two tests, simulating different aspects of the road crossing situation. Analysis of before and after accident statistics showed no significant improvements.

The studies referred to above are only a small sample of the literature on the effects of publicity campaigns, but they are representative. It is clear that, for a majority of the evaluations of publicity campaigns, no effects on traffic safety can be found. This is, as mentioned earlier, partly due to difficulties in evaluating campaigns, but this explanation covers only some studies. For many campaigns there seems to be a genuine lack of effects. The classification presented earlier will be used to determine to what extent this lack of effect can be attributed to ineffective implementation of safety measure, reliance on ineffective mechanisms and/or behavioural adaptation.

It appears that ineffective implementation is a problem with many publicity campaigns. If a campaign is going to produce safety benefits, the target group must at least be reached by the message. This requires effective use of mass media and the perceived relevance of the message by the road user. Exposure to a message is not enough; the road user must think the message is important. According to Andersson (3), the problem can be divided into three parts:

i) The reader must be motivated to read (receive) the material;

ii) The material must clearly communicate to the reader what informational, attitudinal and behavioural changes are necessary;

iii) The reader must make these changes.

It would appear that many campaigns (e.g. 5, 6) fall short of being able to meet these criteria. Even if the three criteria presented by Andersson are met, campaigns can show no effects on safety due to an application of ineffective or invalid mechanisms for accident reduction. The best example of this is the reliance on the assumption that the campaign will change attitudes and that the attitude will produce a behaviour change. The weak link is the belief that attitudinal change will produce a change in behaviour. It has been shown, in a number of studies, that the correlation between attitude and behaviour is very weak for many types of behaviour (see 7 for a review). The "Children in Traffic" campaign presented above (1) is probably an example of this. The campaign produced a change in attitudes towards children in traffic, but this did not reduce accidents. No data were collected to demonstrate behavioural change.

But what are the possibilities of identifying behavioural adaptation in publicity campaigns? Firstly, the literature evaluating different campaigns reveals no clear cases of behavioural adaptation. This could be due either to a genuine lack of adaptive phenomena in this area or to problems with the evaluations in that they did not collect behavioural data. At this stage it might be interesting to speculate on the possibilities of finding adaptive mechanisms in this context.

It will be argued that, when the behaviour of a road user is changed due to a publicity campaign, there is only a small chance of finding adaptive phenomena on the individual level. However, the change in behaviour of the individual road user can very well lead to secondary reactions from other road users, who were not affected directly by the campaign. The major part of adaptive phenomena would, according to this argument, be found for other road users rather than those who have been affected directly by the campaign. The reason for this is that, if a campaign has succeeded in changing the behaviour of road users, then the road users have changed their conceptualization of the task. That is, the road users' idea of normal behaviour (driving, walking, bicycling, etc.) has changed. If road users voluntarily change their behaviour as the result of a campaign, there is little likelihood of adaptive behaviour.

For example, if drivers respond to a campaign about the association between speed, pollution and environmental consequences by driving more slowly, and if this response is due to a true understanding and acceptance of the facts presented in the campaign and not due to an increase in enforcement, then the probability for adaptive behaviour is small. However, for those drivers who have not reduced their speed, the task of driving has changed. They have to make more overtakings, and this could lead to unwanted reactions, such as more irritation, aggressive driving, etc., and an increased risk.

Many safety measures directed towards the traffic environment work in such a way that they make things easier for the road user and therefore provide the opportunity for behavioural adaptation. A successful publicity campaign, on the other hand, works the other way around. It works, in one way or another, by convincing the road user that the old behaviour was more dangerous than originally perceived, or not suitable in some other way, and the new behaviour will, therefore, only put the situation back to an acceptable level.

V.3.   EDUCATION AND TRAINING

In this section the effects of different kinds of road user education and training programmes will be summarized. The literature in this area, which is extensive, seems to suggest that there is a general lack of effect on safety. Very few studies can demonstrate convincingly that education and training reduce accident likelihood.

A good demonstration of this can be seen in a review of 14 studies of the effects of the "Defensive Driving Course" (DDC) (8). According to the authors, the DDC was developed in 1965 as a method for improving driver skills. It was originally developed for professional drivers, but later recommended for use by the general population of drivers and problem drivers. The authors point out that most other post-licensure driver training courses in the USA are similar in length and content to DDC and are used with similar populations. The authors concluded that the only positive effects of DDC on accidents were found in methodologically weak studies. In the methodologically sound studies, no positive effects on accidents could be found. This is a very typical result for evaluation studies in this field in that methodologically sound studies frequently show no, or very small, positive safety effects from education and training.

A report on the SPC-project (Safe Performance Secondary School Driver Education Curriculum Demonstration Project) (9) is an example of a good evaluation of a driver training course. It consisted of a random assignment of 18 000 high school students to one of three groups:

  i) Safe Performance Curriculum (SPC) -- a 70-hour course including classroom, simulation, range, and on-street training;

  ii) Pre-Driver Licensing (PDL) -- a modified curriculum including four-phase instruction, but containing only the minimum training required for the student to obtain a licence; and

  iii) Control -- no formal driver education in the secondary school;

For all students, accident and violation rates were analysed for a two-year period. The results showed that for the first six months of licensed driving, the SPC and PDL groups had a lower accident and violation rate than the control group. However, for the second, third and fourth six month period, no significant differences were found. The analysis of the entire two year period showed no significant differences among the groups.

Butler reviewed the evidence on the effectiveness and efficiency of high school driver education (HSDE) in the USA (10). The conclusion, with respect to effects on safety, was: "As of yet, there are no conclusive studies which are universally accepted as proof that HSDE is or is not an effective driver safety education programme" (10, p.43).

It is, however, normal to find significant improvements on knowledge tests, attitude tests, traffic violations and other intermediary variables following education and training. For instance, after reviewing a number of driver improvement research studies, it was found that traffic violations were reduced, but that there were no reductions in accidents (11). This is not surprising, because many courses attempt to increase safety by affecting these intermediary variables.

The results are similar for the education and training of motorcyclists (12) in that there is no clear evidence that education and training of motorcyclists increase traffic safety. For instance, in an evaluation of the motorcycle rider course in Illinois (13), no differences in accident rate were found between those who had taken a course and those who had not. However, those who took a course made more use of protective equipment, such as helmets, and had, perhaps as a consequence thereof, less severe accidents. It is not clear whether this can be attributed to the course itself or to selective mechanisms, since the design of the study was not experimental. An interesting finding in this latter study was that 44 per cent of those who took the course did not ride a motorcycle in the following year. It is not possible to determine if this was an effect of the course, but if it was it might indicate a possible safety benefit in that riders became non-riders and used safer modes of transport.

In a review of a Canadian motorcycle training programme, no effect on accidents was found (14), but those who had participated in the programme had fewer violations. In a nonexperimental evaluation of the British RAC/ACU motorcycle training scheme (15), efforts were made in the analysis to control for selective mechanisms. It was concluded that the riding performance of the experimental (trained) group was significantly inferior to that of the control (untrained) group, both before and after training.

The results of different programmes for training children to behave safely in traffic show a similar pattern. There are reports of behavioural changes (16, 17), but no clear effects on accidents. A yet unpublished pilot study in Sweden (18), using parents' reports of their children's accidents, indicates almost twice as many accidents per child for children participating in the Children's Traffic Club programme as compared to those not participating. This cannot be explained by differences in exposure (hours in traffic environment), which seems to be equal for the groups, nor can it be explained by differences in "accident proneness"; in fact, the participants seem to have only half the number of non-traffic accidents per child, compared with the non-participants. The author has suggested a number of different selective mechanisms for which there is no control, and that there could be problems with the technique of letting parents report accidents.

It would appear that the behaviour of children can be changed by education and training, but the effects of these behaviour changes on accidents are still in question. One reason for the lack of clarity in the results is the ethical problem associated with using random assignment of children to treatment groups.

There are no clear reasons for the lack of effect on accidents of road user education and training programmes; however, it is likely that the reasons are similar to those for publicity campaigns. The two types of programs, publicity and education, have many similarities for example, they both attempt to convey information about rules and regulations and to use persuasion to change attitudes and behaviour. Therefore, problems of ineffective implementation and reliance on ineffective accident reducing mechanisms are likely common to both education programmes and publicity campaigns.

For road user training, that is, practical training, there seems to be some unique problems which could indicate adaptive mechanisms. The effects of a course in advanced driving for ambulance drivers were reviewed (19). It was found that those drivers who had participated in the course had a higher accident risk than those who had not participated. However, the design of the study was not experimental, so there might be differences other than training between the groups.

A related result was presented by Williams and O'Neill (20), who looked at the accident risks and violations for drivers with competition licence, as compared with those of a matched control group. They found that the race drivers had a higher accident risk and more violations than the control group.

An evaluation of the Norwegian two-phase driver education and training programme that was put into effect in 1979 was carried out (21). This programme introduced three new features: a preliminary-licence period, a dark driving course, and an anti-skid driving course. The preliminary-licence period showed no safety effects, the dark driving course showed a positive effect on accidents in the dark, but the anti-skid driving course showed a negative safety effect. The negative effect of the anti-skid driving course was found not only for accidents on snow and ice, but also for accidents in the dark and for all accidents.

Looking at the effects of a Swiss anti-skid course, Hess and Born (22) found a statistically significant reduction in the overall number of accidents, but failed to find statistically significant differences in the number of personal injury accidents between participants and a control group. However, the study had low statistical power. The participants had about 50 per cent more accidents than the control group, but due to the low number of accidents (26 for participants vs. 17 for the control group) this effect was not statistically significant.

These results (19, 20, 21, and perhaps 22) suggest that a high level of driving skill is associated with a high accident risk. This apparent contradiction could be explained as follows: the belief of being more skilled than fellow drivers increases confidence in one's abilities more than it increases the actual abilities. A high confidence in one's abilities could lead to a more aggressive style of driving that could generate more critical situations. If the driver's increased skill is not in proportion to the increased number of critical situations, then there will be more accidents. Other explantations could be used to explain the effect, but additional research is needed to clarify the processes involved.

V.4. LEGISLATION AND ENFORCEMENT

Legislation covers almost every aspect of the road transportation system since there are rules and regulations for roads, vehicles and road users. It is not the intent in this Chapter to review and evaluate the effects of road transportation legislation in such a broad sense. Rather, this section will review the effects of some examples of road user legislation and try to identify adaptive phenomena. That is, attempts will be made to identify instances where a behaviour has been changed as a response to a change in legislation.

The mere presence of legislation cannot be considered a traffic safety measure. The introduction of a new law, for instance, a seat belt law, requires a number of different actions in order to be useful as a safety measure. First, road user attitudes towards using seat belts must be in favour of the law (publicity campaigns), then the law must be enacted (legislation), the road users must be informed about the law and penalties for violating it (publicity campaigns and education), police enforcement of the law must be of a certain intensity, etc. A new traffic law will not usually have a major effect on road user behaviour if all of the steps are not present. The need for publicity campaigns, education and enforcement is partly a function of how acceptable the law is to road users. If the law is fully accepted, then there is less need for propaganda and law enforcement. If the law is not accepted by road users, the need for these measures is greater, and it is in this case that we would expect to find behavioural adaptation. The traffic laws that have been most accompanied by publicity campaigns and enforcement recently are in the areas of protective equipment (seat belts, helmets), drugs (BAC-level), and speeding. It is therefore natural to look for behavioural adaptation in these areas.

The effects of enforcement on these behaviours is quite well known. It is clear that enforcement has effects, both on behaviour being supervised and on accidents (i.e. 23, 24, 25). What is interesting in this context is whether there are any adaptive phenomena associated with enforcement. The obvious adaptive phenomena on connected with enforcement is the equipment

79

available on the market for drivers to be able to detect enforcement: police radio and radar warning equipment. To equip your car with these devices may be seen as an adaptive measure.

There are data (23) which indicate that drivers are generally well aware of differences in the level of enforcement and alter their travel routes to avoid those that have a high enforcement level. For example, results from a German study indicate that drivers shifted their route from a motorway with an enforced speed limit to one with no speed limit. On the enforced speed route, speed was reduced and the accident ratio decreased 22 per cent while on the alternate route speed increased and the accident ratio increased 29 per cent (23).

Also when it comes to protective equipment, there seems to be possibilities for adaptive phenomena. Evans (27) concludes on the effects of seat belts; "Thus, the results ... taken together, suggest but by no means establish that people compelled to wear seat belts actually reduce their risk taking." This would indicate a positive adaptive phenomenon for the case of seat belt legislation, but this conclusion is not without question.

In a Nigerian study, an increase in both fatalities and injuries was found for a two-year period after the introduction of a law on mandatory use of helmets for motorcyclists (28). The wearing rate was 96 per cent after the legislation. This result seems to indicate a negative adaptive phenomenon as a result of a successful (in wearing rate) helmet law. It was noted that with the helmets on, the riders may have had a false sense of security which would result in greater risk-taking and speeding. However, this result does not seem to be representative of the literature on the effects of helmets. For instance, after looking at injuries following the introduction of a helmet law for moped riders in Sweden (moped = motorcycle with max. 1 hp), no effect was found, although the wearing rate increased from approximately 10-20 per cent to 95 -100 per cent as the law was introduced (29). Looking at fatal motorcycle accidents for eight U.S. states before, during and after the introduction of helmet laws, compared to 8 matched comparison states without helmet laws, a substantial drop in fatal accidents as a function of helmet laws was found (30).

The results on the effects of legislation on protective equipment seem to indicate that there can be adaptive phenomena. But the results also indicate that the behavioural adaptation can have both positive and negative effects on safety. The mechanisms causing adaptation in this context can therefore obviously be different from case to case. It would be interesting to know if the safety effects of these laws correlate with the contents of the publicity campaigns made before and during the introduction of the laws. As was stated in the beginning of this section, legislation by itself cannot be considered to be a safety measure. It is those measures that are taken in order to introduce the law and maintain it that will, or will not, cause adaptation.

V.5. DISCUSSION

Table V.1 provides a summary of the safety effects and possible behavioural adaptations which occurred with the safety measures reported in this Chapter. However, as was discussed in the preceding sections, it is very difficult to present clear evidence for the existence of adaptive mechanisms in the context of safety measures acting directly on the road user. To a large extent, this difficulty stems from the fact that it is difficult (and seldom done) to specify "objective" or physical properties of these safety measures. Education, publicity and legislation can only produce a safety benefit if the road user responds to them. The effect of a new design in the braking system of a car can be described in terms of its effects on stopping distance, vehicle stability, etc., without reference to the driver. However, safety programmes discussed in this Chapter must make reference to the road user in order to describe their effects.

It is difficult to separate the intended effect of the safety measure from the unintended. If the new braking system actually reduces stopping distances, then the intended effect is confirmed. If drivers start to brake later with the new system, there is an unintended effect called behavioural adaptation, and this can be investigated by behavioural observation.

In essence the concept of behavioural adaptation refers to a tendency of road users to take other advantages of safety improving measures than increased safety. That is, if a measure is introduced to increase safety, given that nothing else in the safety system is changed, then road users have a tendency to respond to this measure in a way that gives them other advantages than increased safety. In a strict methodological sense, no such examples have been found for the safety measures in this Chapter. This does not imply that there are no adaptive mechanisms in this context - several have been suggested as hypothetical constructs - but the evaluations do not give the data needed for a clear conclusion. For example, the negative effects of skill training presented earlier strongly indicate behavioural adaptation, but behavioural and psychological data which are needed for this conclusion are unavailable.

Table V.1

SAFETY EFFECTS, INFLUENCE AND DIRECTION OF BEHAVIOURAL ADAPTATION

Safety Measure Adaptation	Safety Effect	Influence of Behavioural Adaptation	Direction of Behavioural Effect
Publicity campaigns	Suggested[1]	Not proven[2]	
Education	Weak positive	Not proven	
Skills training	Possibly negative	Suggested	Negative
Legislation and enforcement	Proven[3]	Not proven	Positive & negative

1. Ranges from positive to no effect
2. Hypothetical effects on collective level
3. Ranges from positive to negative

REFERENCES

1.   TSV. Utvärdering av kampanjen "Barn i trafiken". Trafiksäkerhets-
      verket. Borlänge, 1977.

2.   LALANI, N and HOLDEN, EJ. The greater London "Ride bright" campaign -
      its effects on motorcyclist conspicuity and casualties. Traffic
      Engineering and Control. London, Aug/Sept 1978.

3.   ANDERSSON, JW. The effectiveness of traffic safety materials in
      influencing the driving performance of the general driving population.
      Accident Analysis and Prevention, Vol. 10. 81-94. Oxford, 1978.

4.   ELOFSSON, S. Dataanalys - en fallstudie. Hade trafiksäkerhetsverkets
      kampanj "Barn i trafiken" nagon kortsiktig effekt pa trafiksäkerheten?
      Forskningsrapport 1978:2, Statistiska institutionen, Stockholms
      universitet. Stockholm, 1978.

5.   GLAD, A. Aksjonen "Bedre bilist - 85", Resultater av en evaluering av
      aksjonen. Transportökonomisk institutt. Oslo, June 1986.

6.   DOWNING, CS and SPENDLOVE, J. Effectiveness of a campaign to reduce
      accidents involving children crossing roads near parked cars.
      Laboratory report 986. TRRL. Crowthorne, 1981.

7.   FISHBEIN, M and AJZEN, I. Belief, attitude, intention and behaviour:
      an introduction to theory and research. Addison-Wesley. Reading, MA,
      1975.

8.   LUND, AK and WILLIAMS, AF. A review of the literature evaluating the
      defensive driving course. Accident Analysis and Prevention, Vol. 17,
      No. 6. Oxford, 1985.

9.   STOCK, JR, WEAVER, JK, RAY HW, BRINK, JR, and SADOF, MG. Evaluation of
      safe performance secondary school driver education demonstration
      project. Batelle Columbus Laboratories. Columbus, Ohio, June 1983.

10.   BUTLER, GT. Effectiveness and efficiency in driver education
      programmes. NHTSA Technical Report DOT HS-806 135. US Department of
      Transport. Washington, DC, March 1982.

11.   PECK, RC. Toward a dynamic system of driver improvement programme
      evaluation. Human Factors 18(5), 493-506. Santa Monica, 1976.

12.   FREDEN, S. Om motorcyklar och Trafiksäkerhet. En literaturstudie.
      Unpublished manuscript. VTI. Linköping, 1988.

13.   MORTIMER, RG. Evaluation of the motorcycle rider course. Accident
      Analysis and Prevention, Vol. 16, No. 1. Oxford, 1984.

14. JONAH, BA, DAWSON, NE and BRAGG, BWE. Are formally trained motorcyclists safer? Accident Analysis and Prevention, Vol. 14, No. 4. Oxford, 1982.

15. RAYMOND, S and TATUM, S. An evaluation of the effectiveness of the RAC/ACU motorcycle training scheme. A Final Report. University of Salford, Department of Civil Engineering, Road Safety Research Unit. Salford, Sept. 1977.

16. BENNETT, M, SANDERS, BA and DOWNING, CS. Evaluation of a cycling proficiency training course using two behaviour recording methods. Laboratory Report 890. TRRL. Crowthorne, 1979.

17. ROTHENGATTER, T. The influence of instructional variables on the effectiveness of traffic education. Accident Analysis and Prevention, Vol. 13, No. 3. Oxford, 1981.

18. NOLEN, S. Personal communication. 1988.

19. ERIKSSON, R. Utvärdering av utbildning vid trafikövningsplatser. Uppsala universitet, Pedagogiska institutionen. Uppsala, 1983.

20. WILLIAMS, AF and O'NEILL, B. On-the-road driving records of licensed race drivers. Accident Analysis and Prevention, 6, 263-270. Oxford, 1974.

21. GLAD, A. Fase 2 i Föreropplaeringer. Effekt pa ulykkesrisikoen. TOI Report 0015/1988. Transportökonomisk institutt. Oslo, 1988.

22. HESS, E and BORN, P. Erfolgskontrolle von Antischleuderkursen. bfu-Report 10. Bern, 1987.

23. TFD. Trafikövervakningens langsiktiga effekter pa olyckor och beteenden. Transportforskningsdelegationen 1983:13. Stockholm, 1983.

24. REIN, JG. Virkninger av overvakning, straff, belönning og offentlig informasjon pa trafikanters atferd. Transportökonomisk institutt. Oslo, October 1986.

25. HOMEL, R. Policing the drinking driver. Federal Department of Transport. Report No. CR 42. Canberra, February 1986.

26. Durth, W. Geschwindigkeitsbeschrankung auf Autobahnen - Meinungen, Verhalten, Unfalle. Strasse und Autobahn - Heft 9. 1987.

27. EVANS, L. Human behavioural feedback and traffic safety. Human Factors, 27(5), 555-576. Santa Monica, 1985.

28. ASOGWA, SE. The crash helmet legislation in Nigeria: a before-and-after study. Accident Analysis and Prevention, Vol. 12. Oxford, 1980.

29. TINGVALL, C. Effekter av obligatorisk användning av mopedhjälm. Trafiksäkerhetsverket, analyskontoret. PM nr 30. Borlänge, 1981.

30.   ROBERTSON, LS. Instance of effective legal regulation: Motorcyclist helmet and day-time headlamp laws. Law and Society Review. Vo. 10, No. 3 467-77. Denver, Colorado, 1976.

Chapter VI

REVIEW OF THEORETICAL LITERATURE

VI.1. INTRODUCTION

Road user behaviour has been shown to be very complex in a variety of experimental studies. The purpose of this chapter is to establish a frame of reference around which to organize the information about behavioural adaptation. To do this the chapter contains a review of how various theories explain behavioural adaptation. Each of the theories provides a different explanation for why road users change their behaviour in response to changes in the system. Although not filled with practical information about how to study behavioural adaptation, this chapter should provide a basis for understanding how the concept is incorporated into current theories of road user behaviour and what the current explanations are for behavioural adaptation. In addition, it will provide practitioners with information they need to better understand theories and models.

Theories should not only explain behaviour, but also allow for its prediction. There is a need in road safety to provide prediction of safety benefits, and this can best be achieved by means of theoretical models. The theories reviewed in the chapter were selected because they met three criteria:

-- Presence of a feedback loop;
-- Presence of motivational factors;
-- Explanation for changes in behaviour.

Given these three criteria, and the definition of behavioural adaptation (Chapter II), it is difficult to establish linkages between theories of general and traffic psychology and "behavioural adaptation." Basically, adaptation can be interpreted in the light of the controversy in psychology between cognition of the objective and of the subjective risk. Objective risk can be defined as the product of occurrence probability and seriousness of an event (e.g., accident, police check). Subjective risk can be defined psychologocally as the expectation of a dangerous event with a definite, but unknown seriousness and occurrence probability (1). Such expectations arise when a goal must be reached without the certainty that it can be reached. The more certain a driver feels, the less is his subjective risk.

Risk behaviour is behaviour in situations with a high objective risk. Acceptance of objective risks can be called risk willingness; avoidance of objective risk is called tendency to safety (2). Risk behaviour therefore means that the acting person takes steps to make the occurrence of (objective) risk more or less likely (3). The type of risk behaviour depends on various factors (3, 4, 5):

1. There must be a goal (4);
2. The goal must be based on a certain performance tendency;
3. The attainment of goal requires that an objective risk be taken;
4. The person must also perceive some level of subjective risk.

The conflict between performance and safety tendencies is of special interest to traffic psychology. There is a tendency to avoid objective risk (but not to the extent that risk vanishes altogether), but success in avoiding risk will depend on the processing of cognitions associated with a situation. The absence of a conflict between performance and safety tendencies can be traced to at least three factors:

-- Over-estimation of one's own abilities in the mastering of situations with objective risk;
-- Conscious decision to take an objective risk;
-- Defects in the perception of objective risks.

According to this, adaptation could be interpreted as a process which occurs when the perceived objective risk or the attitude towards objective risk changes and the adjustment leads to a new estimate of subjective risk.

VI.2. ADAPTATION FROM THE POINT OF VIEW OF GENERAL AND SOCIAL PSYCHOLOGY

Theories in general psychology are not able to adequately explain driver behaviour or behavioural adaptation. These theories are either so general that the special aspects of vehicle driving cannot be considered or are so specific that only certain aspects of driver behaviour are touched upon. For example, learning theory can provide explanations of how certain abilities and skills necessary for driving a car can be acquired, and the reception and processing of information while driving can be explained using theories of perception.

Social psychological phenomena also play an important part in road user behaviour in general, and specifically in understanding adaptation. Examples of such phenomena include:

-- Intra-individual processes (attitude research; compare equilibrium models);

-- Inter-individual processes (communication research);

-- Processing of intra- and inter-individual positions (status, etc.);

-- Value systems;

-- Categorisation processes (social representation, groups).

Nevertheless, only a few theoretical frameworks within social psychology can be used to help in the understanding of behavioural adaptation.

For example, attribution theory postulates that the individual attributes the effect of a cause "to whatever condition is present at the time the effect appears and is absent when the effect does not appear" (6, p. 28). The implication is that "behaviour is not immediately released and controlled by stimulating factors of the outside world or of the organism" (7, p. 99). The control of behaviour takes place through a cognitive process because -- despite the basic assumptions -- man tends to ascribe the occurrences he observes to a cause and has a need to rationally understand the causal structure of his surroundings. It is understandable that the traffic participant sees the traffic surroundings in this way and that the processes of information assimilation can partly be explained by attribution theory. Attention must be drawn to the fact that the attribution of one's own capabilities is a source of error due to adaptation. So, for example, the effect of a measure like a technical improvement to a vehicle could be interpreted (attributed) by drivers as improving their personal capability, and this could lead to negative effects on safety.

Adaptation could also be explained under certain circumstances using balance theory. In such cases the need for equilibrium leads to a behavioural change as a reaction to an initial change in behaviour. This could imply a demand for risk or similar phenomena. The adaptational change in risk acceptance in young drivers could be seen as an example in this context. After some experience with a positive adaptational behaviour, young drivers are willing to take more risks and create a balance between the driving experience and the accepted risk.

VI.3. KLEBELSBERG'S MODEL OF OBJECTIVE AND SUBJECTIVE SAFETY

Klebelsberg (8, 9, 10, 11) distinguishes between objective and subjective safety. Objective safety is defined by the physical safety conditions (e.g., static friction), and subjective safety is the experienced safety ("safety feeling"). His model is based on two assumptions:

-- Objective and subjective safety modify each other in the actual situation, i.e., a change in one of the two components can lead to a change in the relationship between the two components;

-- "Behaviour which is adapted (to the traffic situation) presupposes that the objective safety is at least as great as or even greater than the subjective safety, as only in these cases the actual physical limit in a situation can be observed" (10, p. 288).

This model is shown in Figure VI.1. It shows that safety increases on the behaviour level when objective safety increases, without subjective safety increasing to the same extent. Safety diminishes when subjective safety increases, without objective safety increasing in at least the same proportion. For example, the improvement of visibility conditions at a road crossing (higher objective safety) can lead to higher speeds at this crossing (due to the resulting higher subjective safety), and this could be interpreted as an example of behavioural adaptation. Another example is driver behaviour at night after installation of public lighting. Speed measures show that lighted roads lead -- after a short phase of positive adjustment -- to increased speed, which can be interpreted as adaptation.

Figure VI.I. **MODEL OF OBJECTIVE AND SUBJECTIVE SAFETY**

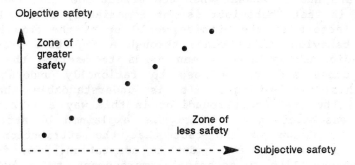

VI.4. WILDE'S THEORY OF RISK HOMEOSTASIS

Wilde asks why drivers are prepared to accept a certain measure of (objective) risk (12). While he does not use the terms "subjective" or "objective" risk, he does try to provide an answer in his theory of risk homeostasis. The theory can be summarised on the basis of the following assumptions (13):

-- Traffic participants always compare the existing measure of subjective risk with the measure of accepted risk which corresponds to their personal level of activation (stimulation requirement).

-- If there is a discrepancy between subjective and accepted risk, the individual tends to eliminate it.

-- The probability of objective risk appears or already exists through the adaptation process.

-- Risk willingness is regarded as an independent variable which determines the accident rate. In its turn, it is stabilised through homeostatic regulation. The accident rate controls the direction and amount of the desired adaptation, but not the risk willingness itself (14).

-- The summing up of the objective risk over all traffic participants results in the accident rate and seriousness for a period of approximately one year.

-- The accident rate, which is measured as a function of the exposure time (15), is constant.

-- The model is based on system-theoretical reflection on theories of equilibrium.

According to Wilde, cognition of risk depends on the possibility of risk perception. The perceived objective risk is estimated and compared with the accepted risk (comparator). The result is the desired caution. The actual caution depends on additional factors such as decision and handling skills. Wilde has grouped these factors into a comprehensive model of homeostasis (Figure VI.2).

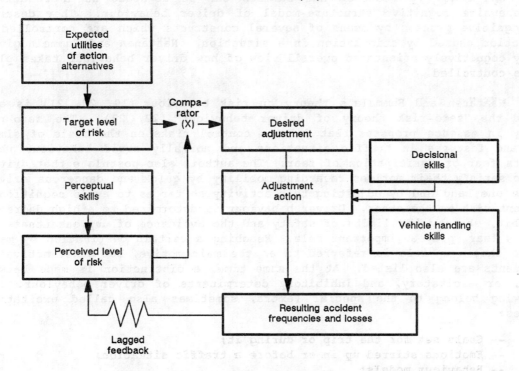

Figure VI.2. **HOMEOSTATIC MODEL RELATING DRIVER BEHAVIOUR, ACCIDENT RATE AND TARGET LEVEL OF RISK (16)**

Wilde's theory has certain similarities to the model by Klebelsberg. Wilde, however, gives a precise prognosis: if measures which reduce the objective risks are taken, there is an increase in safety, as long as the risk acceptance is not influenced. Likewise, safety can be increased in the case of constant objective risk by influencing the driver to take fewer risks. However, these measures are only effective for a short period of time. Wilde expects the estimated and the accepted risks to retain their equilibrium through risk homeostasis. Increases or decreases in safety are only present during the stage of disequilibrium.

Wilde also formulates the "principle of preservation of the accident rate", as follows: "The number of accidents in a certain country depends solely on the accident rate which the population is prepared to tolerate and not on the measures taken in the other areas of this control system, at least not over a longer period of time" (17, p. 147). The principle is not tailored to the individual, but to the social system of the driving population. Thus it becomes difficult to falsify the theory, as general predictions can no longer be formulated precisely. "There is some question as to whether the theory is meaningless (since incapable of testing) or simply false" (18, p. 364). Wilde, however, quotes a considerable number of investigations -- in part his own -- which support the theory. Many of them concern individual behaviour after a change in one of the risk variables. Not all the quoted experiments and analyses were originally designed to test Wilde's hypothesis. Of all the traffic psychology theories, Wilde's is probably the one which is most similar to the process of behavioural adaptation described in this report. A good example of the similarities between behavioural adaptation and risk homeostatis can be seen in the study which reports on the adaptation of taxi drivers to antilock brake systems (see Chapter IV).

VI.5. NAATANEN AND SUMMALA'S THEORY ON RISK BEHAVIOUR

The model by Näätänen and Summala can be regarded as a relatively comprehensive cognitive structure-model of driver behaviour. They describe the cognitive process by means of several constructs which are controlled by the action caused by stimulation in a situation. Näätänen and Summala give a mainly cognitively orientated overall view of how driver behaviour takes place and is controlled.

Näätänen and Summala's theory on risk behaviour (19, 20, 21) is also called the "zero-risk theory of driver behaviour" (22, 23). The zero-risk theory in essence proposes that drivers control risks on the basis of simple cues and features in traffic situations and normally avoid behaviour which elicits fear or anticipation of fear. The authors also postulate that drivers try to satisfy their motives regarding mobility by quick and dangerous driving on the one hand and by adjusting this activity so far as to avoid cognition of accident risk on the other. Driver behaviour is determined to a high degree by habit, whereby the limits of safety and the avoidance of unpleasantness, as well as fear, play an important role. Reaching a certain destination by means of the chosen vehicle is referred to as the main motive, but other motivating components are also listed. At the same time, a distinction is made between extra, or excitatory, and inhibitory determinants of driver behaviour. The following belong to the special (extra, sometimes also called excitatory) motives:

-- Goals set for the trip or during it;
-- Emotions stirred up in or before a traffic situation;
-- Behaviour models;
-- Showing off and the need to prove oneself;
-- Hedonic objectives;
-- Risk for risk's sake.

The most important of the inhibitory motives is the subjective risk and according to the authors, there is a lack of it. The lack of subjective risk can be substantiated by the following:

-- Many forms of behaviour in road traffic indicate a scarcity of subjective risk.

-- In general, the individual does not reduce exposure in traffic to a minimum.

-- Choice and maintenance of the vehicle do not demonstrate observation of the safety aspects.

-- Safety measures based on the concept of subjective risk often miss their target.

-- Experiences by traffic participants do not include elements of subjective risk with regard to accident expectation.

Näätänen and Summala base their theory on the following:

-- That the intensity of subjective risk as cognition of danger is an important motivating factor (i.e., regulator) in driver behaviour; and

90

-- That the subjective risk is not strong enough.

The control loop (Figure VI.3) starts from the stimulus situation to the motor responses. Perception is an active, selective process which is controlled by drivers' motives as well as their experience. Perception triggers expectancies, and a decision is made as to what kind of behavioural change, if any, is needed.

It is postulated, by means of the model, that accidents take place because the subjective risk is too small, the reason being that the driver overestimates his own abilities. This has been substantiated by the results of several opinion polls in which 70-80 per cent of the drivers classified themselves as good or very good drivers. Furthermore, it is indicated that most drivers believe that accidents only happen to others. In addition to these attitudes, perception also plays a role: the estimation of speed is often wrong, depending on the situation, too low, and the physical forces which come into effect in the case of impact wrongly assessed. This tendency is intensified by the subjectively easy task of driving. This is the reason for the driver's tendency to choose higher speeds which should be eliminated. The model implies that the lack of danger cognition leads to a correspondingly riskier style of driving.

Figure VI.3. **FLOW DIAGRAM REPRESENTING THE MOST IMPORTANT FACTORS AND RELATIONSHIPS IN THE DECISION PROCESS AND BEHAVIOUR OF THE DRIVER (21)**

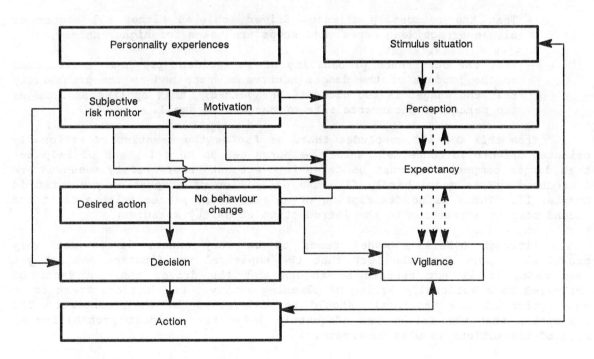

According to the model of Näätänen and Summala, adaptation, as defined in this report, occurs when the driver decides to change an existing action pattern due to a new perception (see subjective risk monitor) or a change in motivation. For example, adaptation after a road has been widened could be explained by a change in the driver's subjective risk monitor (see Chapter III), while a change in driver behaviour following attendance at a skid control course could be explained by a change in motivation [other explanations are also possible (24)].

VI.6. O'NEILL'S DECISION-THEORETICAL MODEL OF DANGER COMPENSATION

O'Neill bases his model of danger compensation on the assumption that the driver a) cannot be considered constant with regard to his driving behaviour, and b) adapts his driving behaviour to changes in the surroundings as a tendency to danger compensation (25).

The theory is based on Taylor's observation that drivers tend to maintain the assumed risk per minute at a constant level (26) and on Wilde's theory of risk homeostasis, which is also based on Taylor. Nevertheless, O'Neill criticizes this basis and tries to explain the phenomena described by these authors in a different way. His theory is not oriented on a compensation theory per se. He derives the "compensation" from the invariable aims of the driver who - assuming he acts "rationally" -- tries to maximise the benefit of the action. During the decision processes necessary for this, the wish to avoid accidents also appears. O'Neill assumes that the driver can correctly assess the situation and his own action. On the basis of mathematic-theoretical reflections, O'Neill predicts:

-- That the rationally oriented driver achieves either all higher or all lower accident rates when steps are taken for higher safety;

-- That the occurrence probability of an accident per hour corresponds to the product of the danger occurrence rate and to the probability that the danger is too close to be avoided; this applies as long as the perceived occurrence rate of dangers is small.

From this O'Neill concludes that, as far as the reaction of rationally oriented drivers is concerned, safety measures can do harm instead of help and that danger compensation must be taken into account before safety measures are introduced. This model hardly fits the definition of adaptation presented in Chapter II. There is no description of an individual process with a first and second step as a reaction to the introduction of safety measures.

Although O'Neill's model seems to be very exact, it is not very practical. Apart from the fact that the empirical verification has not yet been made, it is not certain as to how far the driver can, in fact, be estimated as a rationally acting or planning entity. In addition, there is no description of how "rational" should be understood in this context. The assumption that the driver can adequately judge the accident probability of each of his actions is also uncertain.

VI.7. THE HIERARCHICAL RISK MODEL OF VAN DER MOLEN AND BOTTICHER

Van der Molen and Bötticher developed a hierarchical risk model for traffic participants because of the contradictory results of empirical data of the theories described above (27, 28). The main problem of driver behaviour is that drivers adapt actions on different strategic levels, and on the basis of the environment and psychological processes.

The model is hierarchically structured in terms of a strategic, tactical and operational task level (Figure VI.4). The perception of the physical environment is at each moment influenced by the internal representation of similar situations. It also contains the knowledge of one's own limitations and abilities and the interactions with the environment. The internal representation determines judgemental processes by way of expectations. Motivations of the driver determine the subjective importance of the possible results of behaviour alternatives. The model is a metamodel without explanations of the processes working within the described structure. Therefore it is difficult to show in detail where adaptation could be integrated in the model.

The interaction of safety motivation, expectation and judgement could be relevant in connection with adaptation processes. The authors postulate that, in equally attractive situations on the three different levels, a driver will not choose a more risky alternative when one with less risk is available.

VI.8. EVANS' HUMAN BEHAVIOUR FEEDBACK MODEL

Evans interprets approaches to understanding traffic safety by placing them into three categories (29):

-- "Engineering", meaning that physical changes to the system are considered without addressing possible induced user change;

-- "Economic" or "danger compensation", meaning that users adjust behaviour so that actual safety benefits are less than expected;

-- "Risk homeostasis", meaning that users adjust behaviour to re-establish prior levels of risk taking.

Evans formulates a general human behaviour feedback model in which each of these approaches is included as a special case. The term feedback is chosen "to supersede such terms as danger compensation because feedback can, in principle, be of either sign and of any magnitude" (29, p. 4). Evans assumes that a component of a traffic system is altered in such a way that the engineering safety change is estimated to be SEng. Evans proposes that the actual safety benefit SAct. is not necessarily identical to the engineering change, but is rather related to it by:

Figure VI.4. THE HIERARCHICAL RISK MODEL FOR TRAFFIC PARTICIPANTS OF VAN DER MOLEN AND BOTTICHER

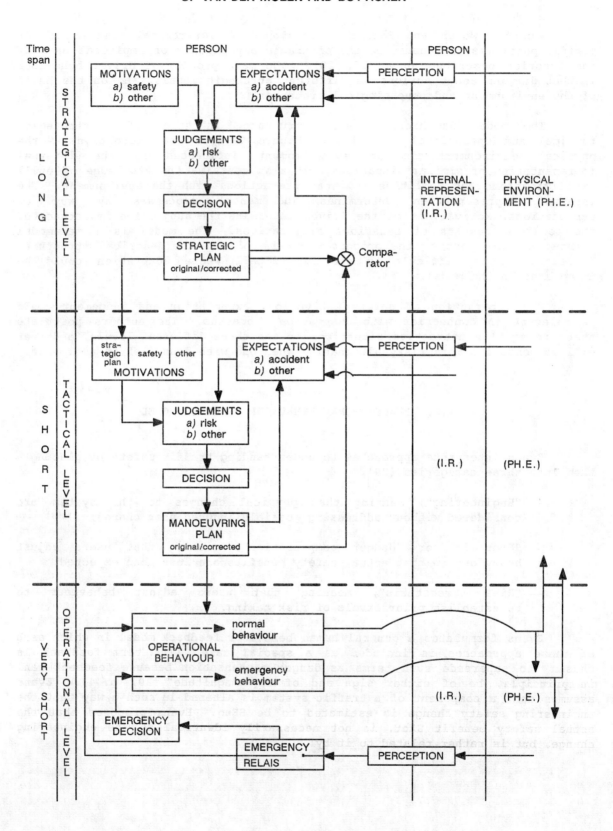

$$\text{SAct.} = (1+f)\ \text{SEng.} \qquad\qquad 1)$$

where f = degree of feedback in the system
and f concerning

engineering	$f = 1$	2)
economic	$-1 < f < 0$	3)
risk homeostasis	$f = -1$	

Evans associates the feedback parameter f with 28 examples of changes made to the road-vehicle-user system taken from the literature. In 15 cases changes were expected to increase safety, and they produced 4 different outcomes: increase in safety more than expected, increase in safety less than expected, no increase in safety, or decrease in safety. In 13 cases changes were expected to reduce safety, providing analogous outcomes: increase in safety, no safety reduction, or decrease in safety less than expected.

Evans suggests that human behaviour feedback is a pervasive phenomenon in traffic systems which may greatly influence the outcome of safety measures. In some cases it may even generate effects opposite in sign to those intended. We need models that take into account the interactive nature of the process as represented by the parameter f.

The feedback model of Evans does not explain the adaptation processes, but rather it is a more specific and numeric description of adaptation and the possible outcomes related to it.

VI.9. MOTIVATION THEORIES

Various authors have tried to theoretically describe the motivational aspects of driving or of unsafe behaviour.

Under the influence of Vroom's concept of expectancy and valency (30), Zink explains a model of unsafe behaviour which could also be of interest in road traffic (31). According to this model, the strength of the motivation for carrying out a certain activity depends on the valency (subjective notion of benefit) of an occurrence and on the expectation of the result of certain activities (behaviour occurrence = valency x expected result; subjective benefit). Safety-oriented behaviour can be expected when the valency for "accident-free" is high. Because of the low likelihood of an accident, however, unsafe behaviour is of instrumental character, as it often leads to results of higher valency (e.g., the saving of time).

In order to make safety-oriented behaviour more attractive, the valency for safety-oriented behaviour would have to be increased (e.g. recognition) and/or positive results in the case of unsafe behaviour would have to be eliminated. The reward (increase of valency) for the road user can take place intrinsically or extrinsically. An intrinsic reward is more promising because a closer connection between reward and action results.

The crucial question in a motivation theory for driver behaviour is, "What valencies become effective during driving or, in other words, what are the stimuli of driving?" (32, p. 34). Apart from the fact that driving makes

95

a certain type of locomotion possible, the question whether -- and if yes, how strongly -- intrinsic motivation plays a role during driving is of special interest in traffic-psychological safety work. Based on an extensive study of literature, a general review of this theme was undertaken and the following observations on driving were made (32):

1. The driver seeks an optimal level of stimulation, so that the activation of the nervous system is neither too weak nor too strong, but an agreeable sensation.

2. In the sense of game behaviour, driving often takes place without having an objective [compare also (33)].

3. Thrill can be generated especially well through driving. The motivating factor in generating fear-inducing situations is the expectation of overcoming this situation.

In terms of "adaptation" these three motivational aspects of driver behaviour could be interpreted as follows:

-- If a safety measure reduces stimulation, e.g. the introduction of a new speed limit, drivers may initially comply with the new measure, but then may adapt their behaviour in order to hold their activation level in equilibrium. The result may be a reduction of the initial effect of the measure.

-- If a safety measure reduces the possibility for the drivers to satisfy their need of game or thrill, they will, after reacting according to the new measure, adapt the behaviour in order to satisfy this need. The result may be a reduction of the initial effect of the measure (see, for example, driving behaviour of young motorbike riders).

VI.10. COGNITIVE THEORIES

The phenomenon of adaptation can also be interpreted in traffic psychology in terms of cognition. Based on an investigation of various accident risk groups, in which measures were taken of the processes of information assimilatione it was concluded that driver's manner of cognitive processing plays an important part in determining the level of accident exposure (34).

Fuller presents an analysis of the driving task from which he developed a threat-avoidance model of driver behaviour based on learning theory (35, 36). With classical conditioning it can be shown that "a distinct preference for delayed avoidance as opposed to anticipatory avoidance responding, that is, a preference for the more risky behaviour" exists. When confronted with a discriminative stimulus for a potential aversive event, a driver's actions depend in particular on the rewards and punishments for alternative responses (35, 36).

In Fuller's model (Figure VI.5.) there is only a connection to adaptation on the immediate action level. Fuller speaks of adjustment-manoeuvres in specific situations to avoid accidents. The "particular pattern of responses followed by a driver... depends on the degree of association (or dissociation) between a discriminative stimulus and a potential aversive stimulus and the rewards and punishments for anticipatory avoidance, competing and delayed avoidance responses" (35, p. 1153).

The threat-avoidance model presupposes that drivers opt for zero risk of accident and make anticipatory avoidance responses. But the theory is not based on a motivation variable. "It is based essentially on a conceptualisation of the driving task as involving learned avoidance responses to potential aversive stimuli and an application of well-established principles of behaviour to the driving situation" (35).

Figure VI.5. **FULLER'S THREAT AVOIDANCE MODEL**

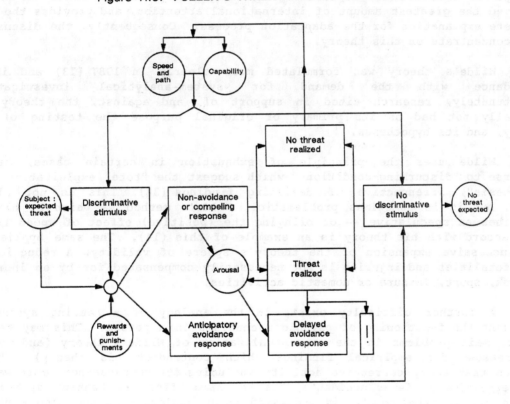

VI.11. DISCUSSION

Although the models presented are in some cases vague, the definitions are not always clear, and most of the theories cannot be falsified in Popper's sense (37), there is evidence within the models for the existence of behavioural adaptation. As there is no one best model or theory, and as they have heuristic value, it is useful to consider all of them in the current context.

One problem with the models is that they are often not clear about whether the behavioural prediction or explanation applies on the individual or the collective level. Also, risk compensation theories generally assume that a balance between objective and subjective risk is required, resulting in constancy of risk, and this would necessitate corresponding cognitions. Risk compensation theories, however, usually do not explain why and which cognitions lead to the expected compensation of objective risk during its change. There is also the problem of how -- driving at an unconscious level (i.e., automatic production of skilled control movements) -- the unknown objective risk can be adequately assessed and exactly compensated in the case of a change. If it can be assumed that the process takes place at a conscious level, then it is not clear why the driver acts in such an irresponsible fashion and rejects additional safety.

The theories discussed in this chapter are interesting, but unfortunately are at times overly general, or only indirectly related to the concept of behavioural adaptation. Wilde's theory is the model which has received the greatest amount of international attention, and provides the most complete explanation for the adaptation process. Consequently, the discussion will concentrate on this theory.

Wilde's theory was formulated more clearly in 1987 (13) and is in accordance with the demand for system-analytical investigation. Unfortunately, research cited in support of, and against, the theory has generally not had as its primary or original purpose the testing of the theory, and its hypotheses.

Wilde uses the principle of exhaustion in certain cases, having recourse to "disturbing conditions" which suggest the "total exploitation of a hypothesis", irrespective of deviating findings (38). This is not always wrong, but it is sometimes problematic. Wilde's method -- which he himself describes as speculative -- of bringing the (positive) effect of speed limits into accord with his theory is an example of this (14). The same applies to the successive expansion of the theory's sphere of validity. A reduction in road fatalities and injuries is not necessarily compensated for by an increase in work, sport, leisure or domestic activities.

A further difficulty exists in the analogy of a heating system to represent the functioning of psychic mechanisms in a person. This may be one of the main problems in the conceptualization of Wilde's theory (and one of the reasons for empirical findings which contradict his theory). Wilde implies that every corrective activity including its consequences (more warmth or, respectively, fewer accidents) has the same effect on heating system and person or, in other words, is processed in an analogous manner, and a person (consistent with the temperature regulation of a heating system) has a constant risk gradient.

The parallel between the two systems (heating system and road user risk acceptance) may not be entirely accurate. The awareness of accident frequency is subjective (too strong, not strong enough, or, by chance, just right in comparison to the objective situation) and has an influence on risk acceptance (in a positive or negative direction). Wilde himself seems to have certain reservations in this respect: "The fact that drivers learn while they are driving is another reason for the already acknowledged imperfection of the analogy of the thermostat which, without being a paradigm proper, appears useful for clarifying the notion of closed-loop control" (39, p. 254). A basic question is: To what extent can theories of equilibrium be used as an adequate basis for the problem in question? Still unsolved is the problem of determining at what point equilibrium is reached. The theory may not define this on the basis of the accident occurrence, but should at least predict the accident level (danger to be circular).

On the empirical level, Wilde lists a number of results which support his theory. Other researchers have also confirmed the model in the areas such as advanced driver instruction (40, 41, 42, 43, 44) and signalisation (45) (the results of this latter investigation speak against the theory of homeostatis). However, later surveys indicate types of behaviour which could be interpreted on the basis of Wilde's model. Several authors have compiled corresponding counter-evidence in refutation of the model (29, 40, 41, 42, 43, 44), which, however, cannot be examined in detail here. Special attention is drawn to the compulsory wearing of seat-belts, which is probably the example quoted most often in this case (see Chapter IV). The same applies to the introduction of speed limits and restrictions regarding the tolerated concentration of alcohol in blood.

According to the theory of risk homeostasis, such measures should not have any effect: "The theory of risk homeostasis posits that the accident frequency/severity compound per time unit of driver exposure is invariant regardless of road geometry" (16, p. 22). It follows that speed limits should result in an increase in accidents, if the prediction is correct, i.e. when the quotient accidents against exposure time (which increases in the case of lower speed for the same distance) remains constant. In this connection Wilde (16) introduces the supposition that the acquired objective safety is compensated through an increase in exposure time. Neither is necessarily the case. Speed limits have shown a positive effect in many countries of the world.

Empirical studies suggest indicate that the underlying psychological mechanisms are probably far more complex than those implied in Wilde's theory. Based on laboratory experiments, it was concluded that "... the constant risk hypothesis appears to hold under different levels of skill and computation time, but fails when task uncertainty is varied" (46, p. 294). And even Aschenbrenner, Biehl and Wurm's very interesting results (see Chapter IV) have to be interpreted very differently (47).

It cannot be denied that adaptation due to "risk compensation" exists (a better name would be "safety compensation"). It seems, however, questionable that these psychological mechanisms thwart the efforts to increase safety on a 1:1 scale. This is not sufficiently substantiated by the risk homeostasis theory and seems, based on the results of the influence of accident prevention measures, to be only acceptable in particular cases. In certain cases, safety measures have provoked negative effects [e.g. "overcompensation" (29)]. It has been argued that certain measures are better than others, i.e., can be effective where others cannot, because whether they attain or do not attain their objective is independent of compensation mechanisms (42, 48). In addition, after a theoretical analysis of the theory of risk homeostasis, it was concluded: "There is no reason why exact homeostasis should be expected to occur as a response of road users to safety hardware improvements: partial compensation seems to be the rule instead" (49, P. 8).

The controversy over Wilde's theory of homeostasis has led many supporters and opponents to study the phenomenon of adaptation. McKenna (42), summarizing current criticism of the theory, presents four assumptions which should be addressed in the theory:

-- People must have a consistent representation of the risk of accident involvement;

-- Following the introduction of a safety measure, the road user can detect the change in risk;

-- People can, over time, completely compensate for changes in accident risk;

-- People cannot be discouraged or prevented from compensating for changes in accident risk.

Wilde (12, 15, 16, 39, 50, 51, 52, 53) presents many arguments opposing his critics. For example, in reply to Shannon (54), Wilde points out that Shannon has confused the average speed of cars and the speed of mobility per capita. Confusion and controversy have also arisen from linguistic and theoretical misunderstandings, as well as from different reference bases used to interpret the few prospective studies which have tested the theory (47, 55, 56).

From a theoretical point of view, the following comprehensive and conclusive assessments can be made:

-- Adaptation mechanisms are phenomena which can be observed in traffic participants and which influence traffic safety in a positive and negative way. Adaptation mechanisms can be seen as elements of various theories in safety research used for predicting driver behaviour.

-- Adaptation mechanisms can be observed on different levels and develop through feedback processes as a function of time.

-- The concept of objective and subjective risk can be taken as a paradigm to understand adaptation mechanisms.

-- Subjective risk interacts with motivational influences on drivers, as well as with perception of driving situations. Motivation is an important element affecting behavioural adaptation.

-- Adaptation mechanisms can be heightened by:

.. Overestimation of one's own abilities while perceiving a situation,
.. Unconscious "decision" or conscious decisions in the choice of higher risks;
.. The inability to perceive the risk of a certain situation (58).

REFERENCES

1. COLBOURN, CJ. Perceived risk as a determinant of driver behaviour. Accident Analysis and Prevention, 2, 131-141. Oxford, 1978.

2. VON KLEBELSBERG, D. Risikoverhalten als Persönlichkeitsmerkmal. Huber. Bern, 1969.

3. COUNT HOYOS, C, KELLER, H and KANNHEISER, W. Risikobezogene Entscheidungen in Mensch-Maschine-Systemen: Arbeitsplatzanalysen in Industriebetrieben. Forschungsbericht zum Projekt HO 182/7. Institut für Psychologie und Erziehungswissenschaft, Technische Universität München, Lehrstuhl f. Psychologie. München, 1977.

4. VOLLMER, GR. Risikoverhalten im innerbetrieblichen Transportsystem Kranführer - Kran. Forschungsbericht No. 120. Bundesanstalt für Arbeitsschutz und Unfallforschung. Dortmund, 1974.

5. SVENSON, O. Risks of road transportation in a psychological perspective. Accident Analysis and Prevention, 4, 267-280. Oxford, 1978.

6. DEUTSCH, M and KRAUSS, R. Theorien der Sozialpsychologie. Fachbuchhandlung für Psychologie. Frankfurt/M, 1976.

7. MEYER, W-U and SCHMALT, H-D. Die Attributionstheorie. In: FREY, D (ed), Theorien der Sozialpsychologie. Huber. Bern, 1978.

8. VON KLEBELSBERG, D. Subjektive und objektive Sicherheit im Strassenverkehr. Schriftenreihe der deutschen Verkehrswacht, Bonn, 1971.

9. VON KLEBELSBERG, D. Psychologische Erklärungshypothesen für das Verkehrsverhalten. Informationen und Mitteilungen. BdP, Sektion Verkehrspsychologie, 9, 3-13. Bonn, 1977.

10. VON KLEBELSBERG, D. Das Moldell der subjektiven und objektiven Sicherheit. Schweiz. Z. Psychologie. 4, 285-294. Bern, 1977.

11. VON KLEBELSBERG, D. Die Bedeutung von subjektiver und objektiver Sicherheit; Fahrerverhalten als Risikoverhalten. In: Verkehrssicherheit, Vorträge anlässlich des Seminars der Forschungsgruppe Berlin, 5/6 November 1981. Daimler-Benz AG, Forschung und Entwicklung. Stuttgart, 1982.

12. WILDE, GJS. The theory of risk homeostasis: implications for safety and health. Risk Analysis, 4, 209-225. New York, 1982.

13. WILDE, GJS. Risk homeostasis theory and traffic accidents: propositions, deductions and discussion of recent commentaries.Ergonomics 31, 441-468. London 1988.

14. WILDE, GJS and KUNKEL, E. Die begriffliche und empirische Problematik der Risikokompensation; eine Erwiderung auf Dr. RD Huguenin. Zeitschrift für Verkehrssicherheit, 1984, 2, 52-61. Darmstadt, 1984.

15. WILDE, GJS. Assumptions necessary and unnecessary to risk homeostasis. Ergonomics, 11 1531-1538. London, 1985.

16. WILDE, GJS. Objective and subjective risk in drivers' response to road conditions: The implications of the theory of risk homeostasis for accident aetiology and prevention. In: Verkehrssicherheit, Vorträge anlässlich des Seminars der Forschungsgruppe Berlin, 5/6 November 1981. Daimler-Benz AG, Forschung und Entwicklung. Stuttgart, 1982.

17. WILDE, GJS. Theorie der Risikokompensation der Unfallverursachung und praktische Folgerungen für die Unfallverhtung. Hefte zur Unfallheltunde, 131, 134-156, Berlin/Heidelberg, 1978.

18. HAIGHT, FA. Risk -- especially risk of traffic accident. Accident Analysis and Prevention, 5, 359-366. Oxford, 1986.

19. NÄÄTÄNEN, R and SUMMALA, H. A model for the role of motivational factors in drivers' decision-making. Accident Analysis and Prevention, 3/4, 243-261. Oxford, 1974.

20. NÄÄTÄNEN, R and SUMMALA, H. A simple method for simulating danger-related aspects of behaviour in hazardous activities. Accident Analysis and Prevention, 1, 63-70. Oxford, 1975.

21. NÄÄTÄNEN, R and SUMMALA, H. Road user behaviour and traffic accidents. North-Holland Publishing Company. Amsterdam, 1976.

22. SUMMALA, H. Modeling driver behaviour: A pessimistic prediction? In: EVANS, L and SCHWING, RC (eds). Human Behaviour and Traffic Safety. New York, 1985.

23. SUMMALA, H. Risk control is not risk adjustment: The zero-risk theory of driver behaviour and its implications. Reports 11. University of Helsinki, Traffic Research unit. Helsinki, 1986.

24. GLAD, A. Fase 2 I FOreropplaeringen - Effekt pa ulykkesrisikoen. Report 0015. Transportökonomisk institutt. Oslo, 1988.

25. O'NEILL, B. A decision-theory model of danger compensation. Accident Analysis and Prevention, 3, 157-165. Oxford, 1977.

26. TAYLOR, DH. Drivers' galvanic skin response and the risk of accident. Ergonomics, 7, 439-451. London, 1964.

27. VAN DER MOLEN, HH. and BOTTICHER, AMT. A hierarchical risk model for traffic participants. Paper presented at the CEC-workshop "Risky decision making in transport operations", Soesterberg. University of Groningen. Haren, 1986 (submitted to Ergonomics).

28.   VAN DER MOLEN, HH. and BOTTICHER, AMT. Risk models for traffic participants: A concerted effort for theoretical operationalizations. In: ROTHENGATTER, JA and BRUIN de RA (ed). Road users and traffic safety. 61-81, Van Gorcum. Assen/Maastricht/Wolfeboro, 1987.

29.   EVANS, L. Human behaviour feedback and traffic safety. General Motors Research Laboratories. Warren, 1984.

30.   VROOM, VH. Work and motivation. Wiley. New York/London, 1967.

31.   ZINK, KJ Arbeitssicherheit als Akzeptanzproblem aus motivationstheoretischer Sicht. Zbl. Arbeitsmedizin, 2, 39-48. Darmstadt, 1980.

32.   COUNT HOYOS, C and VON PUPKA, M. Motivorientierte Aspekte der Verkehrspsychologie. Unfale und Sicherheitsforschung Strassenverkehr, Bd. 7. Bundesanstalt für Strassenwesen, Bereich Unfallforschung. Bergisch Gladbach, 1977.

33.   NAGAYAMA, Y. Characteristics of excessively car-oriented people. In: IATSS. Mobility for man and society. Report of the Symposium on traffic science. International Association of Traffic and Safety Sciences. Tokyo, 1978.

34.   EYE, AV, and HUSSY, W. Zum Beitrag von Variablen der kognitiven Komplexität für die Identifikation verkehrspsychologischer. Risikogruppen. Schweiz. Psychologie, 1, 58-70. Bern, 1979.

35.   FULLER, R. A conceptualization of driving behaviour as threat avoidance. Ergonomics, 11, 1139-1155. London, 1984.

36.   FULLER, R. On learning to make risky decisions. Ergonomics, in press. London, 1988.

37.   POPPER, K. Logik der Forschung. Mohr. Tübingen, 1966.

38.   HOLZKAMP, K. Kritische Psychologie. Fischer. Frankfurt/M, 1976.

39.   WILDE, GJS. Critical issues in risk homeostasis theory. Risk Analysis, 4, 249-257. New York, 1982.

40.   EVANS, L. Risk homeostasis theory and traffic accident data. Risk Analysis, 1, 81-94. New York, 1986.

41.   HUGUENIN, RD. Die Risikokompensationstheorie im Bereich des Strassenverkehrs - kritische Stellungnahme. Referat anlässlich des V. GFS-Seminars Ingolstadt, Gesellschaft für Sicherheitsforschung. Köln, 1984.

42.   McKENNA, FP. Do safety measures really work? An examination of risk homeostasis theory. Ergonomics, 2, 489-498. London, 1985.

43.   FISCHER, H (ed). Evaluation von Weiterbildungskursen für Automobilisten in der Schweiz. Schweiz Konferenz für Sicherheit im Strassenverkehr (SKS). Bern, 1981.

44.   MAREK, J and STEN, T. Traffic environment and the driver: driver behaviour and training in international perspective. Charles C Thomas. Springfield, 1977.

45.   HEHLEN, P, HUGUENIN, RD, and SCHERER, Ch. Verbesserung der Vortrittsverhältnisse bei Verzweigungen von Nebenstrassen. Pilot-Studie; Schweiz. Beratungsstelle für Unfallverhütung (bfu). Bern, 1979.

46.   VEILING, IH. A laboratory test of the constant risk hypothesis. Acta Psychologica, 55, 281-294. North Holland, 1984.

47.   ASCHENBRENNER, M, BIEHL, B and WURM, G. Mehr Verkehrssicherheit durch bessere Technik? Felduntersuchungen zur Risikokompensation am Beispiel des Antiblockiersystems (ABS). (Unpublished). Mannheim, 1988.

48.   McKENNA, FP. Behavioural compensation and safety. J Occupational Accidents, 9, 107-121. Amsterdam, 1987.

49.   JANSSEN, WH and TENKINK, E. Risk homeostasis theory and its critics: time for an agreement. TNO Institute for Perception. Soesterberg, 1987.

50.   WILDE, GJS. Evidence refuting the theory of risk homeostasis? A rejoinder to Frank P McKenna. Ergonomics, 3, 297-304. London, 1984.

51.   WILDE, GJS. La theorie du risque homeostatique: les debats actuels. Proceedings of ATEC 86 - The lack of road safety. Paris, 1986.

52.   WILDE, GJS. Road accident data and risk homeostasis theory: a rejoinder to Harry S Shannon. Submitted to Ergonomics, London.

53.   SHANNON, HS. Road accident data: interpreting the British experience with particular reference to the risk homeostasis theory. Ergonomics, 29, 1005-1015. London, 1986.

54.   SMITH, RG and LOVEGROVE, A. Danger compensation effects of stop signs at intersections, Accident Analysis and Prevention, 2, 95-104. Oxford, 1983.

55.   STREFF, M and GELLER, ES. An experimental test of risk compensation: between-subject versus within-subject analysis. Accident Analysis and Prevention, 20/4, 277-287. Oxford, 1988.

56.   SOMEN, H-D. Risikokognition und -verhalten als Aspekt der Verkehrssicherheit. In: Häcker, H (ed), Fortschritte der Verkehrspsychologie (2). TUV Rheinland GmbH. Cologne, 1987.

Chapter VII

METHODOLOGICAL ISSUES

VII.1. INTRODUCTION

This report is tackling a very complex subject that involves problems of many different kinds. The aim of this Chapter is to examine these problems from a methodological point of view, drawing on the material presented in the previous Chapters.

In this Chapter, the term "methodology" will be used in its broad sense of referring to the study of methods of enquiry, rather than being confined more narrowly to questions of experimental design and methods of data analysis. The wider context covers these questions, as well as those of problem identification, problem definition, and the interpretation and integration of results. Two types of methodological problems can be distinguished: those of a conceptual nature, and those of an empirical nature -- the theory and practice of scientific enquiry. The distinction seems useful in this particular context, given the complexity of the subject matter.

One important problem is the nature of the phenomenon under discussion. For example, it could be argued in some cases that behavioural adaptation is merely a hypothetical construct that has been invoked in the absence of other more plausible explanations (i.e. it is an argument by default). By contrast, Chapter VI has cited those who have argued that it derives from well developed theories of behaviour (e.g. psychological learning theory), and can be used to describe and explain a wide range of behaviours, and behaviour changes.

Though researchers may argue at length about the concept, its existence appears to be taken as almost self-evident by many practitioners. Take, for example, the practice in virtually every developed country of producing an array of standards, warrants, and criteria governing the provision of safety features. Implicit -- and sometimes explicit -- in these is a perceived need to ration the numbers of these features so that they do not "fall into disrepute", in other words, to ensure that behavioural adaptation is not allowed to diminish their safety effects. However, the fact that these criteria vary so greatly among different countries suggests that they depend far more on custom and practice than on general laws of behaviour.

Finally, the existence of behavioural adaptation is widely accepted at an anecdotal level by road users themselves, usually in the context of complaints about the behaviour of other road users. There appears to be a general understanding of the concept, even though it is difficult to define it in other than a general way.

VII.2. CONCEPTUAL ISSUES

Problems of a general nature have been dealt with in Chapter II, so only brief comments will be made here about a few points.

Status of the concept

Although earlier in the report adaptation was put forward as a description of behavioural change in a manner that was deliberately value-free, it seems almost inevitable that behavioural adaptation will be invoked as an explanation for the absence of intended or desired change following the introduction of a safety measure. Many problems in methodology arise from the subtle and often unrecognised shift from description to explanation (accident studies are particularly prone to this failing). It is very important when dealing with an elusive concept like this to ensure that description and explanation do not become confused. The present state of knowledge is such that behavioural adaptation should only be regarded as a descriptive concept.

Absence of effectiveness of new measures and related problems

It is very important that the existence of behavioural adaptation should be based on sound empirical data, and not merely be inferred from the absence of effectiveness of new measures. This latter course is unsound, for most scientific procedures are designed to assess the effects of change, not the absence of those effects. Statistical hypothesis-testing methods explicitly prevent one from drawing any conclusions about the absence of change: the rules merely state that one must "retain the null hypothesis". Even if changes do occur, there are still problems. Without the appropriate data, there are no sound reasons for using behavioural adaptation to describe changes in the system when there are other, and often equally plausible candidates.

Behavioural explanations have been used in the past when accident savings following the introduction of a safety measure were deemed to be different in some way from those that would have been expected or predicted. The problem here is that evaluation studies often leave a good deal to be desired in terms of design and analysis. For example, when Evans (1) reviewed 26 instances of behavioural change, in only seven cases were the results rated as being "fairly clear-cut". Hauer (2) has also drawn attention to the deficiencies of many of the evaluation procedures that have been used in the past.

In some areas, notably education and training, it has been found that the reported effect size reduces with increasing methodological rigour. The review of Lund and Williams of the literature on the Defensive Driving Course is a good example of this (3), as is a more recent review by Struckman-Johnson et al of driver improvement programmes (4). But even if the effect is accepted as real, then there may still be many alternative explanations for it. The poor design or delivery of a safety measure, or problems of selective implementation can diminish the effectiveness of a new measure without the need to introduce behavioural mechanisms. The methodological point here has been made succinctly by McKenna (5): using the absence of change as evidence is like attempting to prove the null hypothesis. Only by incorporating behavioural data into the evaluation process can these problems of the past be overcome.

Nature of methodologies used

Finally, when dealing with this topic, there is the question of not just the nature, but the direction of enquiry. A basic weakness of this field in the past has been that studies have very largely been retrospective in nature, and only recently have prospective studies been undertaken. Prospective studies are needed throughout traffic safety research, and particularly so in this field, because they are more effective at testing hypotheses and at advancing knowledge than are retrospective studies.

VII.3. EMPIRICAL ISSUES

In Chapter II, a definition of behavioural adaptation was put forward. This definition incorporated a number of basic components, such as behaviours, change, inconsistent, intention, safety, and so on. The purpose of this section is to examine the nature of the underlying processes, and to discuss the problems involved.

VII.3.1. Effects of safety measures

The first of these concerns the question of safety measures. It is not always recognised that safety is only one of many interacting components within the transport system. The motives for introducing change into the system are often unclear, and safety as a primary objective is not as common as some would like to think, especially in the engineering field (6). There are also cases where measures that were introduced to achieve non-safety goals have resulted in accident savings. Indeed, one of the most effective safety measures in Great Britain in the last 20 years has been the miniroundabout. This was designed and installed with the intention of increasing capacity and reducing delays at intersections, but an almost unexpected side effect was a significant and sustained reduction in accidents.

The definition of behavioural adaptation used in this report entails that there should be some prediction of the effective of safety measures. This raises the question of the accuracy of prediction. Only a very small proportion of countermeasures in the past have been accompanied by precise estimates of their effectiveness. In many cases, the "expectations" for safety measures have been obtained with the benefit of hindsight (1). Even when attempts are made to specify mechanisms and to predict the accident types that should be reduced, this process can go wrong. One example is the installation of yellow bar patterns on high speed roads, where the hypothesised mechanisms inferred from laboratory studies did not operate in practice. The measure was extremely successful, but the reasons for this are still not clear.

In practice, accurate predictions of the effects of safety measures depend on a knowledge and understanding of the mechanisms affecting behaviour that at present we simply do not have. Even today, many measures are based more on optimism than on understanding. Although it is becoming fashionable to set targets for safety programmes, in reality the state of our knowledge may only allow us to predict with any real confidence that things might improve. Estimates of the scale of any such improvements are more often based on guesswork than on empirical analysis. Partly, this is a statistical problem. The definition of behavioural adaptation put forward in Chapter II referred to the possible effects as lying on a continuum ranging from a clear increase to a clear decrease in safety. Unfortunately, due to the relatively small numbers of accidents and the inherent variability in their distributions, the statistical procedures used in evaluation usually only allow us to be confident about the ends of the continuum, and much of the middle ground remains "not proven". This means that much of the debate tends to be based on speculation rather than established facts.

VII.3.2. Evidence for behavioural adaptation

Perhaps the most important empirical issue that needs to be considered is the nature of the evidence by which behavioural adaptation is established. Effectively, this concerns the relative merits of aggregated accident data versus disaggregated behavioural data. In most discussions of behavioural adaptation, compensation, homeostasis, and so on, the evidence derives to a large extent from changes in accident numbers. This is not just an unrealistic way of assessing behaviour change, it is methodologically unsound. Changes or the absence of changes in accidents cannot be used to infer the existence of behaviour changes.

The problems that have occurred in the past were referred to above with the example of the yellow bar markings on high speed roads. Another good example is the literature on accident migration. Here a statistical phenomenon was identified (7), and behavioural change at an individual level by road users was invoked on an explanation. However, a plausible explanation was subsequently advanced that required no assumptions about behaviour (8). The point here is that if use is to be made of explanations that involve behaviour, then they should be based on behavioural data; accident data alone are unsatisfactory.

VII.3.3. Effects related to time and space

The time and space elements that may be involved in behavioural adaptation can pose serious logical problems. While it would be pleasant in this section to be able to offer practical advice to overcome these problems, this cannot be the case. It must be recognised that the processes involved in behavioural adaptation can operate over both time and space to an extent that is largely unknown.

The spatial element has been discussed at length in the debate over accident migration, but without arriving at any clear conclusions. If it is argued that drivers will change their behaviour in response to an intersection improvement, should one look for this change at the next intersection, the one after that, or at intersections in general? If delays are introduced by installing a new junction control, will drivers make up the time on the downstream link? The literature provides little or no guidance on this point. The temporal element is more worrying from a methodological point of view. If it is argued that the effectiveness of some safety measures declines over time, how far can this principle be taken, given that the longer the timespan the "noisier" the data becomes and the more difficult it becomes to reach clear and unambiguous conclusions?

These are all empirical questions to which there will be many different answers depending on the nature of the measures under consideration. But these answers can only be obtained by carrying out evaluation studies that will be more detailed and complex than has usually been the case in the past. Of necessity, these evaluation studies must include the systematic observation of behaviour as well as the consideration of accident data. In the present state of knowledge, the only practical and sensible advice is to go out and collect empirical data.

From this brief discussion of empirical issues, it can be seen that the definition of behavioural adaptation that was advanced in Chapter II is not without its methodological problems. However, it is important to stress that these problems are not insuperable given a willingness to engage in research rather than debate. But it is equally important to stress that the research must be well planned and well directed if it is to overcome the problems.

VII.4.   LESSONS FROM THE LITERATURE

As stated earlier, one of the purposes of this Chapter is to draw lessons from the material that has been provided by the literature reviews in the preceding Chapters. This will be done mostly in the form of making brief observations rather than detailed assessments, since the reviewers have drawn attention themselves to most of the important methodological points in their comprehensive reviews.

VII.4.1. Highway safety measures

This is such a vast subject that Chapter III has inevitably needed to be selective. To do this, two criteria were used. First, that the measures studied should be visible to the driver and should influence vehicular control. Second, that as far as possible the measures should have a continuing effect on the driving task.

The criterion of success for these environmental measures has in the majority of cases been accident changes, but other behavioural variables -- especially speed -- have also been considered. One point that comes across strongly is the difficulty involved in treating intermediate variables as predictors of accident change. For example, the installation of edgelines was associated with increased driving speeds, but was not associated with a corresponding increase in accidents. Again, the behaviour-accident relationship is a complex one. Chapter III shows that an increase in speed does not necessarily lead to a safety problem, since it depends on where the increase takes place. These findings tend to highlight our general lack of knowledge about the interaction between the road user and the environment, particularly where road markings are concerned. Nonetheless, the overall tone of the Chapter is an encouraging one, in that it suggests that if behavioural adaptation does occur, it does not nullify the net safety benefits.

VII.4.2. Vehicle measures

Chapter IV, which dealt with the vehicle, has given a thorough review of the data and the issues involved, and such a review of changes in vehicle design should provide the ideal testing ground for the influence of behavioural adaptation. Here there should be the possibility of controlled experiments on performance/safety trade-offs while holding road user factors constant. This proved to be the case. Six types of measure were examined; conclusive evidence for behavioural adaptation was found for three of them, it was suspected in one, and no good evidence was found in the case of the other two. However, much of the analysis is of changes in accidents, and when behaviour change has been investigated the results have usually been more ambiguous. Given the relevance of vehicle measures to the discussion of behavioural adaptation, there are some important methodological points in this Chapter that merit further discussion.

The first of these concerns the assessment of the "package" of primary safety measures and improved performance characteristics. It is reported that the safety gains are often not realised, and that accident rates are higher for high performance vehicles. The question at issue here is the nature of the measure being introduced. If a vehicle is bought (and probably sold) because of its performance characteristics, the fact that it also incorporates improved safety features may well be of little concern to its user. When safety is a secondary consideration, the identification of behavioural adaptation as a general process becomes problematic, particularly as there is probably a high degree of interaction between the characteristics of individual drivers and the characteristics of the vehicles they choose to drive.

The second topic concerns high mounted brake lights. The results here were mixed, with the positive effects on safety found in the American studies not being confirmed in a large German study. That investigation found no overall effect of high mounted brake lights on accident rates, but did find a higher than expected number of accidents where both vehicles were fitted with the measure. Behavioural adaptation was advanced as an explanation for this, based on interviews with a representative sample of German motor vehicle drivers, however no behavioural observations were made (headways adopted in freeflowing traffic would seem an obvious measure here). The point of methodological interest here is the need to be aware of the possibility of novelty effects when only a small proportion of vehicles is equipped with a particular measure. As numbers increase, there is the possibility of further behavioural change. Indeed, the author reports that there is a view in some quarters that the safety benefits of high mounted brake lights are decreasing. There is therefore a need for the monitoring of such measures to be continued on a regular basis, and not just after their first introduction.

The discussion of studded tyres provides a good example of a measure that has been subject to comprehensive evaluation, incorporating measures of knowledge, behaviour, exposure, and accidents. This measure has long been cited as an example of adaptation or compensation because of a well known Swedish study which showed that drivers with studded tyres drove faster in icy conditions than did drivers with conventional tyres. This is interpreted as negative behavioural adaptation because the full safety benefits are not achieved. There are two problems with this, however. One is that it is not possible to specify in advance what the "full" benefits should be, and so it can only be assumed that they are not being achieved as a result of the slight increase in speed. The second is that it is most improbable that studded tyres are perceived as a "pure" safety measure by drivers. The tyres give mobility as well as safety, and it is somewhat naive to expect speeds to remain unchanged. The methodological point here again is the nature of the measure. Even if introduced solely as a safety measure, anything that patently provides mobility benefits must expect to have them used. The adaptation to this measure is unsurprising, since safety is probably seen as being a secondary issue here; the important and interesting result is the net safety benefit in both icy and non-icy conditions.

The final topic for comment is the assessment of antilock braking systems (ALS). This has been advanced as strong evidence, not just for behavioural adaptation, but also for risk homeostasis theory (9). The design of the Munich study reported in Chapter IV was of a high standard, with random allocation of drivers to experimental and control groups, "blind" ratings by observers, and the use of attitudinal, behavioural, and accident data. Nonetheless, the results of the study are not particularly clear-cut. The behavioural data showed little difference between the two groups. The main finding from the accident study was that there was no difference in accident rates between drivers equipped with ALS and those without. There were also some rather puzzling features in the accident analysis, for example, ALS was associated with fewer blameworthy accidents, but with more parking accidents. The first of these is in line with predicted safety effects, but the second is difficult to explain in terms of adaptation. Overall, the study cannot be regarded as conclusive and unambiguous evidence for adaptation or risk compensation for methodological reasons. First, there is the problem of estimating the predicted effect when the measure is only intended to operate in critical situations. The second is that the original report set up the hypothesis that ALS did not reduce accidents, and claimed that behavioural adaptation in the form of risk compensation occurred because it was not possible to disprove the hypothesis. This is a logically dubious procedure. In addition, where effects might be expected to be small, statistical power becomes a critical issue, and the relatively small numbers involved reduce the probability of identifying real differences. Thirdly, there is the problem of general inability. The study was conducted among taxi drivers, who might well have different attitudes, motivations, and behaviours from the non-professional drivers who make up the bulk of the driving population. As Wilde (9) has quite properly pointed out, what holds for Munich taxi drivers may not hold for other groups of people.

The material presented in this Chapter clearly points to the need for a better understanding of the interactions within the system, this time between road user and vehicle, but probably also with the environment as well. At present, we do not know enough about these matters.

VII.4.3. Road user measures

Chapter V has looked at "direct" safety measures, that is, those that aim to bring about change in the road user without any change in the vehicle or in the environment. Three main groups of measures were considered: publicity, education, and enforcement. This broad grouping raises the first methodological problem -- that of defining the issue under discussion. For example, the installation of edgelining is a relatively standardized procedure, and -- as pointed out in the Chapter -- one studded tyre is much like another. However, publicity programmes vary enormously in quality of content and effectiveness of implementation. This makes it difficult to reach any general conclusions about effectiveness and about the possible effects of behavioural adaptation, not least because the objectives are rarely specified in behavioural terms. There is a certain irony here, in that it is the group of measures that aims to act directly on the road user that is the least explicit in formulating its behavioural intentions.

Then again, it is not even clear on logical grounds whether behavioural adaptation can apply to "direct" measures, since they are designed to act on road users and to make them aware of behavioural change. The Chapter notes that "direct" safety measures have no physical properties other than the effects they aim to achieve. But normally these intended effects are phrased in such general terms that it is extremely difficult to distinguish between unintended effects and intended ones.

If Chapter V provides little in the way of support for behavioural adaptation, it is largely because the evaluation procedures have not produced the evidence needed in order to draw clear conclusions. Three possible explanations are advanced in the Chapter for the lack of effect of a road user safety measure:

-- The inadequate design of the measure;

-- The inefficient implementation of the measure;

-- Behavioural adaptation by the target group.

It proved extremely difficult to choose between these three explanations, and the final verdict on behavioural adaptation was a fully justified "not proven".

VII.5. DISCUSSION

When drawing conclusions and offering recommendations for further research, it is necessary to repeat again that this report is dealing with a topic that is more easily recognised than defined. While there are lessons that can be learned from this exercise, it needs to be recognised that the literature that has been reviewed only rarely provides clear and unambiguous directions for future action.

It would, for example, be helpful to be able to indicate where and when behavioural adaptation is likely to take place. Some guidance can be offered on this point, particularly regarding the notion of freedom of action. This is discussed at some length in the conclusion section of Chapter IV, and will not therefore be repeated here.

The evidence indicates that the more readily available the opportunities for substituting performance improvements for safety improvements, the more likely it is that these opportunities will be taken. But this conclusion is so general as to be of limited practical value, saying little more than that if given better roads and better vehicles, drivers will travel at higher speeds. This in itself is unremarkable; it is the effect on safety that is crucial, and is where the evidence is difficult to interpret.

The reasons for this have been alluded to several times in this Chapter already. In brief, the problem lies in the fact that the design, implementation, and evaluation of safety measures in the past has not been carried out in such a way as to provide a body of knowledge about how safety measures work, or do not work. To understand behavioural adaptation requires an understanding of the processes of behavioural change, and it is this that has been so lacking in the past, where too much discussion has been carried out at the statistical level, and not enough research at the behavioural level. Without more behavioural research, the prospects of solving the problems associated with adaptation are slim.

This report deals with a contentious topic, and one that is accompanied at times by intense and at times vociferous debate. Because of this, it is vital that evaluation procedures lead to unambiguous results. To be capable of throwing more light on the phenomenon of behavioural adaptation, the evaluation process should include the following:

i) A clear specification of the objectives of the safety measure being introduced;

ii) A description of the behavioural mechanisms by which the objectives are to be achieved;

iii) A design that provides suitable for extraneous factors;

iv) The collection of both short term behavioural data and long term accident data;

v) Sample sizes that are adequate to identify reliably small effects;

vi) Analysis procedures that are appropriate to the design of the study;

vii) A design that allows the results to be generalised to the population as a whole, and not just to specific sub-groups.

The final point is the need for more prospective studies. The retrospective analysis of historical accident data is not an adequate or satisfactory way of proceeding in the search for solutions to the problems of behavioural adaptation. What are needed are clear predictive hypotheses and well designed procedures for testing them, as well as a commitment to long term evaluation and monitoring of safety measures.

In conclusion, it should be stressed that this emphasis on improved evaluation procedures should not be seen simply as a defensive measure designed to assess the effects of behavioural adaptation. In the longer term, positive and sustained benefits can be expected if a better understanding of the operation of the road-vehicle-user system leads to a better formulation and implementation of safety measures.

REFERENCES

1. EVANS, L. Human behaviour feedback and traffic safety. Human Factors, 27, 555-576. Santa Monica, California, 1985.

2. HAUER, E. The effect of traffic safety measures: what we have learnt and what we don't know yet -- background paper. In: Proceedings of the Evaluation 85 Conference. ONSER, Arcueil, 1985.

3. LUND, AK and WILLIAMS, AF. A review of the literature evaluating the defensive driving course. Accident Analysis and Prevention, 17, 449-560. Oxford, 1985.

4. STRUCKMAN-JOHNSON, DL, LUND, AK, WILLIAMS, AF and OSBORNE, DW. Comparative effects of driver improvement programs on crashes and violations. Accident Analysis and Prevention. 21(3), 203-215. Oxford, 1989.

5. McKENNA, FP. Do safety measures really work? An examination of risk homeostasis theory. Ergonomics, 28(2), 489-498. London, 1985.

6. GRAYSON, GB. Behavioural studies and the evaluation of safety measures. In: Proceedings of the Evaluation 85 Conference. ONSER, Arcueil. 1985.

7. DOYLE, AJ and WRIGHT, CC. Accident "migration" after remedial treatment at accident blackspots. Traffic Engineering and Control, 25, 260-267. London, 1984.

8. MAHER, MJ. Accident migration -- a statistical explanation? Traffic Engineering and Control, 28, 480-483. 1987.

9. WILDE, GJS. Risk homeostasis theory and traffic accidents: deductions and discussion of dissension in recent reactions. Ergonomics, 31(4), 441-468. London, 1988.

Chapter VIII

CONCLUSIONS AND RECOMMENDATIONS

The purpose of the report was to examine evidence of road user behaviours which occur in response to road safety programmes and to assess the potential impact of these behaviours on the safety benefits obtained from the programmes. The term used to describe the behaviours of interest in the report is behavioural adaptation.

-- Behavioural adaptations are those behaviours which may occur following the introduction of changes to the road-vehicle-user system and which were not intended by the initiators of the change.

-- Behavioural adaptations occur as road users respond to changes in the road transport system such that their personal needs are achieved and as a result, they create a continuum of effects ranging from a positive increase in safety to a decrease in safety.

The report was also prepared as a result of the contention by some road safety researchers that behavioural adaptation can nullify the safety benefits intended by road safety programmes. Controversy surrounding this contention has led to a polarisation of opinion about the effectiveness of road safety programmes. The report has been prepared so as to provide a description of behavioural adaptation, as opposed to an explanation, with the intention of reducing the polarisation of the issue.

The broader acceptance of behavioural adaptation as a real phenomena, independent of the various explanations, should lead to additional research on the effects of behavioural adaptation on road safety programmes and the process by which it occurs. It is anticipated that a better understanding of the process of behavioural adaptation will assist in the development of more effective countermeasures.

Seven objectives were established for the report:

1. To define behavioural adaptation;

2. To review the issues associated with the phenomena;

3. To review research which describes the responses of road users to road safety programmes directed at the highway system, the vehicle and road users;

4. To review the theories of road user behaviour which might explain the phenomena;

5. To discuss methodological issues associated with research about the phenomena;

6. To provide conclusions about the existence, extent, and magnitude of the phenomena;

7. To provide recommendations for the consideration of the phenomena in research.

The first five of these objectives have been achieved in the preceding Chapters. In Chapter II, the general issues of behavioural adaptation were discussed along with a more detailed discussion of the definition. Chapters III through V provided reviews of research which had shown how drivers adapt their behaviours to changes in the road transport system. Chapter VI provided a review of theories of road user behaviour. Chapter VII provided a discussion of some of the methodological issues to be considered when conducting research involving the potential for behavioural adaptation. The remaining objectives are achieved in the two sections of this Chapter which follow.

VIII.1. CONCLUSIONS

The research reviewed indicates that behavioural adaptation to road safety programmes does occur although not consistently. The magnitude and direction of its effect on safety cannot be precisely stated. There is evidence that behavioural adaptation is more readily identified following vehicle and road system changes than following the implementation of educational programmes.

The studies reviewed suggest that behavioural adaptation generally does not eliminate the safety gains from programmes, but tends to reduce the size of the expected effects. Therefore, the data do not support the argument that road safety programmes are ineffective. However, the negative effects of behavioural adaptation remain a concern, and there is a need to explore systematical factors which affect behavioural adaptation in order to better understand and predict its effect on road safety.

In Chapter III, which discussed the effect of behavioural adaptation on changes implemented to improve safety on highways, it was concluded that behavioural adaptation could be observed for such measures as increased lane width, increased shoulder width, and edge line markings. There was some evidence that behavioural adaptations by drivers might influence the magnitide of safety benefits obtained from freeway lighting and increased sight distances. These behavioural adaptations did not entirely eliminate the safety benefits achieved by the countermeasures. It was also concluded that there was no evidence of behavioural adaptation for centre line markings and arterial lighting.

Behavioural adaptation to changes in vehicle safety systems were identified in Chapter IV. The literature reviewed provided evidence of behavioural adaptation to improved vehicle design (including suspension systems, etc.), studded tyres and antilock brake systems, and may have been present for high mounted brake lights and seat belts. There was no evidence, in the research reviewed, of behavioural adaptations to daytime running lights. It was also argued, in this Chapter, that road users must be able to perceive changes in order for behavioural adaptation to occur. In general, changes which increase drivers' mobility are more likely to produce behavioural adaptations.

Behavioural adaptation affecting road users was the third area reviewed in the report (Chapter V) and its effect on road safety was the least clear. The majority of studies reviewed in the Chapter lacked behavioural data making it impossible to determine, for them, if behavioural adaptations were occurring. There was some evidence that specialised driver training might lead to overconfidence, resulting in a negative influence on safety. In addition, there was limited evidence that indicated that in some cases road safety legislation and its enforcement could lead to unintended changes in road user behaviour, which could in turn, have a negative impact on the safety benefits derived from the measure. It was pointed out that many educational programmes did not specify the mechanisms by which changes would occur, and therefore, appropriate measures of outcome were not collected. As a result, it was impossible to distinguish between alternative explanations (e.g. poor delivery, in appropriate approach, or behavioural adaptation) for the results obtained.

In Chapter VI models and theories of driver behaviour which incorporated a feedback mechanism were reviewed. Within the models the explanations for behavioural adaptation varied, but there was support for the influence of behavioural adaptation on drivers. General models of behaviour were lacking in specification, and were therefore of limited value in the discussion of road user behaviour. Further development of theories of driver and road user behaviour are needed for a better understanding of road user behaviour, and to assist in the development of an organised body of research. The development of useful theories is important for the development of effective countermeasures because theories are needed to organise and explain empirical results.

The data used to demonstrate the existence of behavioural adaptation have been taken from reports not specifically designed for this purpose. However, these are the only data currently available, and therefore there was no alternative to using them. In most cases evaluations were based on accident data, with only a limited amount of behavioural data being available. It is anticipated that in the future more behavioural data will be collected in the process of conducting evaluations of road safety programmes.

It would appear, from the research reviewed, that there has generally been a lack of effort to develop an understanding about the process of behavioural change which accompanies road safety programmes. The behavioural change process is complicated, and the reliance on outcome measures such as accident fatality rates has often precluded the inclusion of data collection which would permit the study of the change process. With a more complete understanding of the process of behavioural adaptation it may be possible to predict how safety programmes will influence the behaviour of road users.

VIII.2. RECOMMENDATIONS

The recommendations follow from the material presented in the preceding seven Chapters of the report. They were developed to provide concrete suggestions for road safety administrators, programme planners, and researchers. it was the intent of the report to encourage further discussion and understanding of behavioural adaptation in road safety. The recommendations should stimulate new research on road user behaviour and it is hoped that this will result in an increased level of safety in the road transportation system.

1. The potential effect of behavioural adaptation should be considered in the development and evaluation of all road safety programmes.

2. Behavioural data should be collected and used as a supplement to fatality and accident data when conducting evaluations of road safety programmes. The behavioural data will provide information on the process of change in road user behaviour and an understanding of this process will assist in the prediction of the potential effectiveness of future programmes.

3. Researchers must be careful to collect behavioural data which are likely to be sensitive to the behavioural adaptations of road users. Researchers should collect a variety of potential indicators of behavioural adaptation rather than relying on only one or two such measures.

4. The potential for behavioural adaptation affecting a safety measure should be considered in estimating the costs and benefits of safety programmes. Programmes with minimal adaptation may be more effective, in the long run, than those which produce large initial safety gains, but also produce adaptations that eliminate the gain.

5. There is a need for additional research to identify, define, and specify relevant methodologies for measuring indicators of behavioural adaptation. This work could lead to the development of standard indicators which would be used for specific types of road safety programmes. As well, this research could identify subgroups of the road user population who are more prone to behavioural adaptation.

6. The possibility of behavioural adaptation must be specifically studied as part of a research project if it is to be used to explain the results. That is, it is not acceptable to invoke the explanation of behavioural adaptation if behavioural data have not been collected. Specifically, one cannot infer adaptation from accident and fatality statistics.

7. Research should be conducted on how road users who are not drivers adapt to changes in the road transport system. To date, most research relevant to behavioural adaptation has been concerned with the driver, but other road users, for example, pedestrians and cyclists, also modify their behaviour in response to changes imposed on them by road safety planners, and road and vehicle system designers.

8.	There is a need for long term research into behavioural adaptation to determine how behaviours change over many years. With long term data changes to the safety of the road transport system can be monitored by changes in behaviour as well as through the use of more traditional accident and fatality statistics.

9.	There is a need for further development of theories of road user behaviour to assist in the understanding and prediction of behavioural adaptation. At the same time there is a need for those conducting evaluations of road safety programmes to incorporate theory testing in their research to provide a basis for the development of theory.

10.	Behavioural adaptation is likely to occur in response to non-safety changes (e.g. highway improvements, improvements in vehicle performance) in the road transport system, and it is possible that these adaptations will result in a reduction in the level of safety. Efforts should be made to encourage planners and designers to consider the potential negative safety implications of behavioural adaptation resulting from their activities.

11.	There is a need for multi-national research which will assist in understanding cultural differences which influence behavioural adaptation. it is quite possible that a safety programme will succeed in one country, but not in another because of cultural differences which influence behavioural adaptation.

LIST OF GROUP MEMBERS

Chairman: Mr. B.A. Grant

AUSTRALIA

Mr. A. COLLINGS
Principal Research Officer
Federal Office of Road Safety
Department of Transport
GPO Box 594
CANBERRA ACT 2601

BELGIUM

Mrs. DE VRIEZE
Institut Belge pour
 la Sécurité Routière
Chaussée de Haecht, 1405
1130 BRUXELLES

CANADA

Mr. B. GRANT, Ph.D.,
Head Human Factors
Road Safety Directorate
Transport Canada
Canada Build.
344 Slater St.
OTTAWA, Ontario K1A ON5

DENMARK

Mr. H. JOHANSEN
Danish Council of
Road Safety Research
Ermelundsvej 101
DK-2820 GENTOFTE

Mrs. L. HERSTEDT
Danish Ministry of Transport
The Road Directorate
Road Data Laboratory
Stationsalleen 42
Postbox 40
DK-2730 HERLEV

FINLAND

Prof. O. MANNINEN
University of Tampere
Faculty of Medicine
Department of Public Health
P.O. Box 607
SF-33101 TAMPERE

FRANCE	Mr. G. MALATERRE Chargé de recherche INRETS - LPC Autodrome de Linas 91310 MONTLHERY
	Mr. S. LASSARRE Chargé de Mission INRETS - DERA B.P. 34 2, avenue du Gl Malleret-Joinville 94114 ARCUEIL CEDEX
GERMANY	Mr. I. PFAFFEROTT Bundesanstalt für Strassenwesen Postfach 100 150 Brüderstrasse 53 D-5060 BERGISCH GLADBACH 1
IRELAND	Mr. A. CURRAN Head Road Safety Section An Foras Forbartha St Martin's House Waterloo Road DUBLIN 4
JAPAN	Mr. Y. MOTODA Head of Traffic Safety Division Public Works Research Institute Ministry of Construction Asahi 1-Branch, Tsukuba-shi Ibaraki-ken, 305
THE NETHERLANDS	Mr. P. LEVELT Institute for Road Safety Research SWOV Duindoorn 32 2262 AR LEIDSCHENDAM
NORWAY	Mr. T. BJORNSKAU Department of Traffic Safety Norwegian Institute of Transport Economics P.O. Box 6110 Etterstad N-0602 OSLO 6
SPAIN	Mr. L. NUNES GONZALEZ Direccion General de Trafico c/Josefa Valcarcel 28 28071 MADRID
SWEDEN	Mr. R. JOHANSSON Chief Researcher VTI S-581 01 LINKÖPING

SWITZERLAND	Mr. R. HUGUENIN Bureau Suisse de Prévention des Accidents (BPA) Case postale 2273 Laupenstrasse 11 3001 BERNE
UNITED KINGDOM	Mr. G. GRAYSON Behavioural Studies Unit Transport & Road Research Laboratory Old Wokingham Road CROWTHORNE, Berks RG11 6AU
UNITED STATES	Mr. T. MAST Traffic Systems Division (HSR-10) Federal Highway Administration Department of Transportation Turner-Fairbank Highway Research Center 6300 Georgetown Pike McLEAN, VA. 22180
	Mr. J. HEDLUND Director Office of Driver & Pedestrian Research (NRD-40) National Highway Traffic Safety Administration 400 7th Street, S.W. WASHINGTON, D.C. 20590
OECD	Mr. C. MORIN Ms. M.D. GORRIGAN

Rapporteurs of the various chapters of the report were: B. Grant, G. Grayson, R. Huguenin, H. Johnson, T. Mast, I. Pfafferott.

Members of the Editorial Committee were: B. Grant, G. Grayson, R. Huguenin, H. Johansen, R. Johansson, O. Manninen, T. Mast, I. Pfafferott, OECD Secretariat.

WHERE TO OBTAIN OECD PUBLICATIONS
OÙ OBTENIR LES PUBLICATIONS DE L'OCDE

Argentina – Argentine
Carlos Hirsch S.R.L.
Galeria Güemes, Florida 165, 4° Piso
1333 Buenos Aires
Tel. 30.7122, 331.1787 y 331.2391
Telegram: Hirsch–Baires
Telex: 21112 UAPE–AR. Ref. s/2901
Telefax:(1)331–1787

Australia – Australie
D.A. Book (Aust.) Pty. Ltd.
648 Whitehorse Road (P.O. Box 163)
Vic. 3132   Tel. (03)873.4411
Telex: AA37911 DA BOOK
Telefax: (03)873.5679

Austria – Autriche
OECD Publications and Information Centre
4 Simrockstrasse
5300 Bonn (Germany) Tel. (0228)21.60.45
Telex: 8 86300 Bonn
Telefax: (0228)26.11.04
Gerold & Co.
Graben 31
Wien I   Tel. (0222)533.50.14

Belgium – Belgique
Jean De Lannoy
Avenue du Roi 202
B–1060 Bruxelles
          Tel. (02)538.51.69/538.08.41
Telex: 63220 Telefax: (02)538.08.41

Canada
Renouf Publishing Company Ltd.
1294 Algoma Road
Ottawa, Ont. K1B 3W8 Tel. (613)741.4333
Telex: 053–4783 Telefax: (613)741.5439
Stores:
61 Sparks Street
Ottawa, Ont. K1P 5R1 Tel. (613)238.8985
211 Yonge Street
Toronto, Ont. M5B 1M4 Tel. (416)363.3171
Federal Publications
165 University Avenue
Toronto, ON M5H 3B9 Tel. (416)581.1552
Telefax: (416)581.1743
Les Publications Fédérales
1185 rue de l'Université
Montréal, PQ H3B 1R7 Tel.(514)954–1633
Les Éditions La Liberté Inc.
3020 Chemin Sainte-Foy
Sainte-Foy, P.Q. G1X 3V6
          Tel. (418)658.3763
Telefax: (418)658.3763

Denmark – Danemark
Munksgaard Export and Subscription Service
35, Norre Sogade, P.O. Box 2148
DK–1016 Kobenhavn K
          Tel. (45 33)12.85.70
Telex: 19431 MUNKS DK
          Telefax: (45 33)12.93.87

Finland – Finlande
Akateeminen Kirjakauppa
Keskuskatu 1, P.O. Box 128
00100 Helsinki   Tel. (358 0)12141
Telex: 125080 Telefax: (358 0)121.4441

France
OECD/OCDE
Mail Orders/Commandes par correspon-
dance:
2 rue André-Pascal
75775 Paris Cedex 16   Tel. (1)45.24.82.00
Bookshop/Librairie:
33, rue Octave-Feuillet
75016 Paris   Tel. (1)45.24.81.67
          (1)45.24.81.81
Telex: 620 160 OCDE
Telefax: (33–1)45.24.85.00
Librairie de l'Université
12a, rue Nazareth
13602 Aix-en-Provence Tel. 42.26.18.08

Germany – Allemagne
OECD Publications and Information Centre
4 Simrockstrasse
5300 Bonn   Tel. (0228)21.60.45
Telex: 8 86300 Bonn
          Telefax: (0228)26.11.04

Greece – Grèce
Librairie Kauffmann
28 rue du Stade
105 64 Athens   Tel. 322.21.60
Telex: 218187 LIKA Gr

Hong Kong
Swindon Book Co. Ltd
13–15 Lock Road
Kowloon, Hong Kong   Tel. 366.80.31
Telex: 50.441 SWIN HX
Telefax: 739.49.75

Iceland – Islande
Mal Mog Menning
Laugavegi 18, Postholf 392
121 Reykjavik   Tel. 15199/24240

India – Inde
Oxford Book and Stationery Co.
Scindia House
New Delhi 110001   Tel. 331.5896/5308
Telex: 31 61990 AM IN
Telefax: (11)332.5993
17 Park Street
Calcutta 700016   Tel. 240832

Indonesia – Indonésie
Pdii-Lipi
P.O. Box 269/JKSMG/88
Jakarta12790   Tel. 583467
Telex: 62 875

Ireland – Irlande
TDC Publishers – Library Suppliers
12 North Frederick Street
Dublin 1   Tel. 744835/749677
Telex: 33530 TDCP EI Telefax : 748416

Italy – Italie
Libreria Commissionaria Sansoni
Via Benedetto Fortini, 120/10
Casella Post. 552
50125 Firenze   Tel. (055)645415
Telex: 570466 Telefax: (39.55)641257
Via Bartolini 29
20155 Milano   Tel. 365083
La diffusione delle pubblicazioni OCSE viene
assicurata dalle principali librerie ed anche
da:
Editrice e Libreria Herder
Piazza Montecitorio 120
00186 Roma   Tel. 679.4628
Telex: NATEL I 621427
Libreria Hoepli
Via Hoepli 5
20121 Milano   Tel. 865446
Telex: 31.33.95 Telefax: (39.2)805.2886
Libreria Scientifica
Dott. Lucio de Biasio "Aeiou"
Via Meravigli 16
20123 Milano   Tel. 807679
Telefax: 800175

Japan– Japon
OECD Publications and Information Centre
Landic Akasaka Building
2–3–4 Akasaka, Minato-ku
Tokyo 107   Tel. 586.2016
Telefax: (81.3)584.7929

Korea – Corée
Kyobo Book Centre Co. Ltd.
P.O. Box 1658, Kwang Hwa Moon
Seoul   Tel. (REP)730.78.91
Telefax: 735.0030

**Malaysia/Singapore –
Malaisie/Singapour**
University of Malaya Co-operative Bookshop
Ltd.
P.O. Box 1127, Jalan Pantai Baru 59100
Kuala Lumpur
Malaysia   Tel. 756.5000/756.5425
Telefax: 757.3661
Information Publications Pte. Ltd.
Pei-Fu Industrial Building
24 New Industrial Road No. 02–06
Singapore 1953   Tel. 283.1786/283.1798
Telefax: 284.8875

Netherlands – Pays-Bas
SDU Uitgeverij
Christoffel Plantijnstraat 2
Postbus 20014
2500 EA's-Gravenhage Tel. (070)78.99.11
Voor bestellingen: Tel. (070)78.98.80
Telex: 32486 stdru Telefax: (070)47.63.51

New Zealand –Nouvelle-Zélande
Government Printing Office
Customer Services
P.O. Box 12–411
Freepost 10–050
Thorndon, Wellington
Tel. 0800 733–406   Telefax: 04 499–1733

Norway – Norvège
Narvesen Info Center – NIC
Bertrand Narvesens vei 2
P.O. Box 6125 Etterstad
0602 Oslo 6
          Tel. (02)67.83.10/(02)68.40.20
Telex: 79668 NIC N Telefax: (02)68.19.01

Pakistan
Mirza Book Agency
65 Shahrah Quaid-E-Azam
Lahore 3   Tel. 66839
Telex: 44886 UBL PK. Attn: MIRZA BK

Portugal
Livraria Portugal
Rua do Carmo 70–74
1117 Lisboa Codex   Tel. 347.49.82/3/4/5

**Singapore/Malaysia
Singapour/Malaisie**
See "Malaysia/Singapore"
Voir "Malaisie/Singapour"

Spain – Espagne
Mundi-Prensa Libros S.A.
Castello 37, Apartado 1223
Madrid 28001   Tel. (91) 431.33.99
Telex: 49370 MPLI Telefax: 575.39.98
Libreria Internacional AEDOS
Consejo de Ciento 391
08009 –Barcelona   Tel. (93) 301–86–15
Telefax: 575.39.98

Sweden – Suède
Fritzes Fackboksföretaget
Box 16356, S 103 27 STH
Regeringsgatan 12
DS Stockholm   Tel. (08)23.89.00
Telex: 12387 Telefax: (08)20.50.21
Subscription Agency/Abonnements:
Wennergren-Williams AB
Box 30004
104 25 Stockholm   Tel. (08)54.12.00
Telex: 19937 Telefax: (08)50.82.86

Switzerland – Suisse
OECD Publications and Information Centre
4 Simrockstrasse
5300 Bonn (Germany) Tel. (0228)21.60.45
Telex: 8 86300 Bonn
Telefax: (0228)26.11.04
Librairie Payot
6 rue Grenus
1211 Genève 11   Tel. (022)731.89.50
Telex: 28356
Maditec S.A.
Ch. des Palettes 4
1020 Renens/Lausanne Tel. (021)635.08.65
Telefax: (021)635.07.80
United Nations Bookshop/Librairie des Na-
tions-Unies
Palais des Nations
1211 Genève 10
          Tel. (022)734.60.11 (ext. 48.72)
Telex: 289696 (Attn: Sales)
Telefax: (022)733.98.79

Taïwan – Formose
Good Faith Worldwide Int'l. Co. Ltd.
9th Floor, No. 118, Sec. 2
Chung Hsiao E. Road
Taipei   Tel. 391.7396/391.7397
Telefax: (02) 394.9176

Thailand – Thalande
Suksit Siam Co. Ltd.
1715 Rama IV Road, Samyan
Bangkok 5   Tel. 251.1630

Turkey – Turquie
Kültur Yayinlari Is-Türk Ltd. Sti.
Atatürk Bulvari No. 191/Kat. 21
Kavaklidere/Ankara   Tel. 25.07.60
Dolmabahce Cad. No. 29
Besiktas/Istanbul   Tel. 160.71.88
Telex: 43482B

United Kingdom – Royaume-Uni
H.M. Stationery Office
Gen. enquiries   Tel. (071) 873 0011
Postal orders only:
P.O. Box 276, London SW8 5DT
Personal Callers HMSO Bookshop
49 High Holborn, London WC1V 6HB
Telex: 297138 Telefax: 071.873.8463
Branches at: Belfast, Birmingham, Bristol,
Edinburgh, Manchester

United States – États-Unis
OECD Publications and Information Centre
2001 L Street N.W., Suite 700
Washington, D.C. 20036-4095
          Tel. (202)785.6323
Telex: 440245 WASHINGTON D.C.
Telefax: (202)785.0350

Venezuela
Libreria del Este
Avda F. Miranda 52, Aptdo. 60337
Edificio Galipan
Caracas 106
          Tel. 951.1705/951.2307/951.1297
Telegram: Libreste Caracas

Yugoslavia – Yougoslavie
Jugoslovenska Knjiga
Knez Mihajlova 2, P.O. Box 36
Beograd   Tel. 621.992
Telex: 12466 jk bgd

Orders and inquiries from countries where
Distributors have not yet been appointed
should be sent to: OECD Publications
Service, 2 rue André-Pascal, 75775 Paris
Cedex 16.
Les commandes provenant de pays où
l'OCDE n'a pas encore désigné de dis-
tributeur devraient être adressées à : OCDE,
Service des Publications, 2, rue André-
Pascal, 75775 Paris Cedex 16.

OECD PUBLICATIONS, 2, rue André-Pascal 75775 PARIS CEDEX 16
PRINTED IN FRANCE
(77 90 01 1) ISBN 92-64-13389-5 - No. 45203 1990